101 Birds

of

Belize

Carolyn M. Miller

Illustrations by Fernando Zavala and Alejandro Grajal
Forewords by Craig Lee and Philip Balderamos
Introduction by Alejandro Grajal

Front Cover: The beautiful painting of the Harpy Eagle
by Alejandro Grajal represents the 101st bird for the
second edition of *100 Birds of Belize*.

Published for the Belize Audubon Society by *Producciones de la Hamaca,*
    Caye Caulker, Belize, Central America
Second Edition
ISBN 978-976-8142-19-1

First Edition:
100 Birds of Belize by Carolyn Miller, 1995
Published by American Bird Conservancy, The Plains, Virginia, USA

The cover painting of a Harpy Eagle is by Alejandro Grajal.

The black and white drawings on pages 1 - 15 are by Alejandro Grajal.

The color paintings are by Fernando Zavala. Those on pages 19, 20, 29, 30, 31, 32, 34, 36, 38, 41, 42, 48, 52, 53, 58, 65, 68, 69, 79, 82, 91, 96, and 101 were commissioned by Rainforest Expeditions for the Tambopata Project and used by permission. The others were commissioned by the National Audubon Society.

The protected areas map on p. 17 is by Judy Lumb using data from Jan Meerman <biological-diversity.info> with permission.

The **Belize Audubon Society** is a non-governmental membership organization dedicated to the sustainable management of our natural resources through leadership and strategic partnerships with stakeholders in order to create a balance between people and the environment.

The mission of the **National Audubon Society** is to conserve and restore natural ecosystems, focusing on birds, other wildlife, and their habitats for the benefit of humanity and the earth's biological diversity.
    <www.audubon.org/bird/IAP>

Producciones de la Hamaca is dedicated to:
—Celebration and documentation of Belize's
    rich, diverse cultural heritage,
    —Protection and sustainable use of Belize's
        remarkable natural resources,
        —Inspired, creative expression of Belize's
            spiritual depth.

Dedication

This book is dedicated to the founding officers and directors of the Belize Audubon Society (BAS), formed in February 1969. BAS has done much to promote conservation and excite interest in the spectacular wildlife and wild lands found in this beautiful country.

BAS Founding Officers:
James A. Waight, President
Dora Weyer, First Vice President
Louis Lindo, Second Vice President
Lydia Waight, Secretary
Albert S. Grant, Treasurer

BAS Founding Directors:

Meg Craig
Ronald L. Clark
Henry Fairweather
Magnus Halcrow
Col. Martin Hastings
Winston Miller
Esther Pendergast
Gil Rosado
Normal Staines
Father Leo Weber, S.J.
Father Charles Woods
W. Ford Young

Today, BAS board, staff, members, and friends carry BAS forward in the 21st Century as one of the most influential and preeminent conservation organizations in the region. (*see p. 151*)

Belize Audubon Society
P.O. Box 1001
12 Fort Street
Belize City
Belize, Central America.
Tel: +501 223-5004/4987/4988
Fax: +501 223-4985
E-mail: base@btl.net
Website: belizeaudubon.org

Acknowledgments

An undertaking like this book can never be accomplished alone. Although it focuses on Belize's birds, it is multinational in many respects, involving many people in the USA, Venezuela and Belize vitally interested in the conservation of birds in the Neotropics. I want to thank ornithologist, artist and long-time friend, Alejandro Grajal, for being the catalyst for a second edition. The stunning cover and black and white drawings are his. Alejandro and Ricardo Stanoss put me in contact with artist Fernando Zavala through his agent, Guillermo Knell. It is thanks to them that we have the lovely illustrations for 101 Birds that enhance the Second Edition so beautifully.

I am very grateful to the National Audubon Society (NAS) for providing funding for this project through the W.K. Gordon Jr. Family Foundation. NAS's Craig Lee and Greg Butcher have been helpful and enthusiastic in partnering for the Second Edition. Andrea Kraljevic of NAS oversaw the many details and liaisons necessary to help make the Second Edition a reality.

Judy Lumb (Producciones de la Hamaca) lent her considerable expertise, skills and talent to the editing, layout and publishing of this book. She is grateful to Jan Meerman for his devoted work on the Biodiversity and Environmental Resource Data System of Belize <biodiversity.bz>, which provided the data needed to prepare the map of protected areas in Belize.

Long-term, greatly appreciated supporters include Barry and Dixie Bowen, and Connie and Jerry Holsinger. Bruce Miller, my partner in all things, as always, gave his encouragement, assistance and support to this project.

Carolyn M. Miller

Gallon Jug, Belize

Foreword from the National Audubon Society

Belize opened my eyes to the joys of tropical birds and their environments. And that experience set me on a different course that has shaped my life. This book is a milestone along that course.

As a tourist from a northern part of the USA, all the sights, sounds, smells and tastes of Belize were as foreign to me as the humid warmth the first time I visited. The country was full of surprises for every sense. But, together with the wonderful Belizean people, it was the glorious array of birds that captivated me night and day.

What I would have given to have this book when I crept out of my room at first light to investigate the incredibly strange calls emanating from a tree festooned with gigantic hanging, woven nests. It would have helped me to quickly figure out that I was seeing my first Oropendula. Instead I had to study the immense Peterson volume *Birds of Mexico and Central America* to find this amazing creature.

Even though Belize now has its own bird guide, a sure sign that a country is renowned for its avian treasures, it is still a challenge for most people to identify common bird species from among the more than 550 that have been found in Belize.

A book like this one can be like a first visit to a new locale. Even if the place is familiar to you, the text and images can serve as a pathfinder to a new way of "seeing" one's natural environs. Knowledge of birds, or any other part of the world around you, pulls back the curtain on the drama that is everywhere. Much like the beginning of a play, the stage is revealed and you can witness the action and understand the characters. Carolyn Miller and Belize Audubon offer this newly revised version of *101 Birds of Belize* so that citizens and visitors will have the opportunity to see the exciting scene that I witnessed on my first trip.

On that trip I also learned an important lesson. It can be paraphrased as "economics rule ecosystems". Belize has the good fortunes of abundant forests, numerous rivers, healthy fisheries and fertile soils. As a result, it has been able to provide for its relatively small population. But where the population has grown quickly or the commercial demands on the natural world are too great, even Belize's resources can be depleted.

v

Belizeans, like people everywhere, want to achieve sustainable, dignified livelihoods. Sometimes these motivations appear to be at odds with the goals of retaining the jungles, estuaries, shorelines and farms on which birds and other animals and plants depend. In Belize, I had the good fortune to see how protecting places for birds and other creatures also benefits human residents. This concept is a fundamental component of the work of Belize Audubon Society, and now of the International Alliances Program, that I direct, for National Audubon Society, which is based in the USA.

Together, our two organizations have produced this book to foster and promote the potential for Belizeans and their marvelous birds to share a prosperous future. When more citizens can see and recognize and appreciate the unique animals with which they share in their country, the more likely it is that they can all thrive. Birds and Belizeans together make the country special. We look forward to protecting both.

Craig Lee, Director
Vice President and Director
International Alliances Program
National Audubon Society

Foreword from the Belize Audubon Society

Since its inception in 1969, the Belize Audubon Society has reached out to hundreds of Belizeans, young and adult, and introduced them to the natural wonders of Belize. The Society's pioneering efforts have fostered greater awareness of Belize's ecology, natural history and significantly, our birds.

In 1995, with the support of many partners, Carolyn Miller released the first edition of this book, *100 Birds of Belize*. As the first widely available publication on the avifauna of Belize, it received high acclaim and was much in demand. The first edition certainly achieved their aim of educating and motivating readers to conserve the Belizean environment through knowledge of birds and the important ecological niche they occupy. The cadre of ardent Belizean birders now extends to all six districts of the country.

101 Birds of Belize carries on the effort to maintain this rich tradition. *101 Birds of Belize* will satisfy repeated requests for a reprint of the author's earlier publication. This volume is updated and expanded to include the Harpy Eagle, highlighting Belize's efforts to reintroduce this species, and features an updated bird list and protected areas map as well as new illustrations.

We highly recommend this book. The splendid images and detailed text will surely provide many hours of pleasure to field and armchair birders alike. Congratulations once more to Carolyn Miller!

As with the first edition, *100 Birds of Belize*, Carolyn Miller has donated her time and expertise to write this book and keep it in print for perpetuity with all proceeds benefiting the Belize Audubon Society for bird conservation and education. BAS is very grateful to Carolyn Miller!

Philip Balderamos
BAS Member and former President
Winner of the 2008 BAS James A. Waight Conservation Award

Introduction

The unexpected torrential rains of the previous night had left the forest floor soggy and the air muggy. Now in mid-morning, the early bird chorus had subsided, a few flycatchers called from the canopy, and the cicadas were working hard toward the apotheosis of their noon crescendo. We were walking a trail among spectacular caves and forests of St. Hermans's Blue Hole National Park, smack in the middle of Belize.

Then, in the shaded silence of the trail, an unexpected sound, that at first was hard to identify: First, a sound that seemed like someone ripping a long cloth, followed by a resounding staccato CLAP! We stopped to mute our steps, and more ripping cloth and staccato claps sounded near and far, all around us. The thick vines and brush at the edge of the trail hindered our sight. We were trying to find the source of this weird sound, until Patrick Scott, Jr., our park ranger with the Belize Audubon Society, with the patient amusement and friendliness displayed by Belizeans, pointed us to a tiny white bird with a black head and a stubby tail, more like a white feathered ball than anything else.

Soon we spotted several of these White-collared Manakins, nervously jumping up and down in the thick vines. We stumbled upon a "Lek" of singing male White-collared Manakins. Like the Bird of Paradise in New Guinea or the Cock of the Rocks in South America, these Manakins select a place in the forest where all the males strut their stuff and perform these elaborate dances and songs, with the hope of attracting the much more subdued and quiet females. Indeed, a drab green female showed up among the branches, and we could feel the testosterone-meter going through the roof, as all 15 or more males started going crazy, jumping, singing and flipping their wings at incredible speeds to make that un-bird-like ripping sound.

Wonderful evolutionary story, I thought, as I lowered my binoculars. I smiled back at Patrick, and looked around, soaking in the beauty of this magical moment. This perfectly nice jewel, Blue Hole, is just a small part of a remarkable conservation achievement by the people of Belize. With a characteristic ever-humble approach, Belize is one of the countries in the world with the proportionally largest commitment to conservation, deeply rooted in national pride.

Having nearly 50% of the country in some sort of natural protection status is no small feat for any country, much more for a small country as Belize, without economies of scale or large markets. Indeed, Belize is one of the world's leaders, leaving a progressive path toward conservation that even wealthier countries would only dream about. A group of dedicated conservationists and their Belizean organizations have been major actors in this remarkable achievement. The Belize Audubon Society is one of the oldest and largest of these groups, and they manage nine national parks and reserves on behalf of the Government of Belize. Other groups, large and small—from the organization Programme for Belize to creative private land owners, to local community-based organizations—help conservation in their own Belizean proud way.

Belize is a remarkably convenient destination to see lots of tropical birds. Outside visitors may have the idea that to visit tropical rainforests or coral reefs you have to travel very far, communicate with non-English speakers, or survive obscure tropical diseases. Not true, Belize is closer than you might think. Just two hours from Houston or Miami, you can literally have breakfast in the USA and watch Rufous-tailed Jacamars before dinner. Everyone speaks English in a wonderful kaleidoscope of Mayan, West Indian, Garifuna, Creole, Chinese and British cultures. The atmosphere is definitely laid back—out with ties and high heels, in with binoculars and hiking shoes (or snorkels and fins!).

Driving just a few hours you can visit spectacularly diverse habitats, like the vast lagoons of Crooked Tree, where, if you are quiet and have a good guide, you may spot the secretive Agami Heron, perhaps the most beautiful heron in the world. Crooked Tree is a smaller version of the Pantanal or the Everglades, a place where tens of thousands of ducks and coots spend the winter, and home to one of the largest populations of Jabiru storks in Central America. The Jabirus are huge, and when they fly close by, you cannot stop but compare them with the wingspan of a small Cessna.

If you visit the Tapir Mountain Nature Reserve in the winter, you may be surprised to see dozens of migratory Black and White warblers, Redstarts and many other wintering North American migratory birds feeling right at home among the bromeliads and tropical vines.

Many people come to Cockscomb with the very unlikely hope to see jaguars, but most will experience a close encounter with the spectacular velvety contrast of the Crimson-collared Tanager, or the languid call of the Violaceous Trogon.

And in the middle of impossibly crystalline turquoise waters of Half Moon Caye, the noisy colonies of Frigatebirds and Red-footed Boobies will remind you of how most of the Caribbean really looked before most of it was turned into beach resorts.

This book is the second edition of Carolyn Miller's *100 Birds of Belize*. I have known Carolyn for many years, and she is one of Belize's outstanding ornithologists, dedicated to introducing many Belizeans and visitors to her beloved birds. I hope you enjoy this book, which highlights some of the common, most interesting or outright beautiful birds of Belize. These are not all the birds—there are more than 550 species in Belize—but this is a good introduction in a handy package.

So whether you are proficient at distinguishing different species of Myiarchus Flycatchers or telling female hummingbirds apart, or if otherwise this is your first time pointing binoculars at our feathered friends, you will find that Belize brings a hard-to-find combination of bird diversity, cultural diversity, friendliness, convenience, and true conservation ethos.

If you are a first time visitor or a native Belizean, I hope this book brings the birds of Belize closer to your heart. If Carolyn's book inspires your return, you will be supporting the noble efforts that Belizeans have made to conserve their natural heritage for all future generations.

Alejandro Grajal
Senior Vice-President for
Conservation, Education and Training
Chicago Zoological Society

Contents

Birds and People

Perhaps as long as people have been on the earth, we have admired birds for their beauty, delighted in their song, envied their flight. Ancient peoples revered birds and incorporated them into their religious ceremonies as well as their daily rituals.

Although people have historically enjoyed and utilized birds, we have caused them serious problems in the world we all share. Some of the most serious of these problems are destruction of birds' habitat and food resources, over-hunting, and pollution.

Similarities between people and birds, although perhaps not at once obvious, are several. We are both bipedal (two legged), we both have a keen sense of color (most mammals are color blind), our senses of smell are poorly developed, and both parents invest a great amount of time and effort in raising their young.

Humans are not alone on this planet. We share it with countless wild creatures. Visible and easily seen in almost any part of the world, birds are as close as our gardens and as far away as the most inhospitable environments in the world. Belize has been blessed with a rich diversity of bird life that is mostly intact due to extensive and varied habitats, and relatively low human population and development pressures. However, this situation is changing.

What is a Bird?

We see birds all around us. They occur on every continent, every sea, every climate and yet, what are they exactly? They have a backbone like mammals, reptiles and fish, so they are vertebrates. They are warm blooded like mammals, but do not have fur or hair. Although many can swim, they are very different from fish.

It is believed that birds evolved from dinosaurs. In 1860 in Bavaria, fossilized slate was discovered bearing both feather

1

imprints and skeletal imprints. The skeleton looks very reptilian with a long lizard-like tail and three fingered claw-like appendages from the forelimbs. Recent fossil finds, particularly in China, have added more credence to this idea.

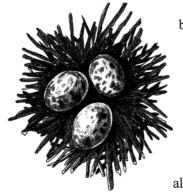

Birds lay eggs as did dinosaurs. But birds are uniquely clothed in feathers, something which no other animal has. Feathers protect birds from the elements, like rain, and keep them warm. Feathers are also part of what makes flight possible. They are light and aerodynamic and must be kept in top condition. Feathers and wings, combined with light hollow bones allow birds to fly. The ancestors of birds were capable of flight; today most, but not all, birds can fly. Birds are unique then, in having feathers and the ability to fly.

Each bird species may be known by several different names depending on the region and the languages spoken by the people there. As you read about the different species in Belize, you will see an English name, a Spanish name, and sometimes Mayan and Creole names.

To get around the confusion of many different names, scientists have assigned internationally agreed upon Latin names to each species. This gives one commonly accepted scientific name for each bird. The first name refers to the genus and the second, to the species, and all scientific names are italicized. For example:

Common names: Scientific name:
Great Blue Heron   *Ardea herodias*
Full-pot
Garzón Azulado

Bird species with similar characteristics, that is birds classified in the same genera, are also members of a larger family. For example, there are many different species of parrots, but all belong in the same family, the *Psittacidae*. Ducks and geese belong in another family (*Anatidae*), hummingbirds in yet another (*Trochilidae*). There are many different levels of classification, ranging from broad to specific.

2

Adaptations

As you become more observant of birds, you will notice that they are well designed for what they "do" in life. A hummingbird has a long slender bill that allows it to probe deeply into a flower to feed on nectar. Frigatebirds, a common sight along Belize's coast and cayes, can glide for hours on long strong wings, beautifully designed for long distance travel with little effort. A duck's feet are webbed which allows it to paddle through water efficiently. Herons have long legs that they use to wade in search of food. A woodcreeper has special spines on the ends of its tail feathers which prop it in place as it scurries along the sides of trees in search of insects which make up its diet. Eagles, hawks and owls have strong toes and sharp talons to hold their prey and sharp bills for tearing their food. These are just a few of the special characteristics of birds that help them to live successfully.

Such special features, so necessary to a bird's way of life, are called "adaptations". By carefully observing a bird, and noting especially their bill, feet, and wings, you will have some idea of how it lives.

Bird Behavior

What an animal does during its life is known as its "behavior." An animal is concerned with feeding, avoiding predators, mating and rearing young. This could generally be called "survival." Each bird species has certain behaviors it carries out during its lifetime to ensure its own survival and that of its species.

For example, each bird species needs to feed in order to survive, and part of each day is taken in this activity. For hummingbirds it means searching for special flowers preferred for nectar. For hawks it may mean soaring several hours seeking prey with their sharp eyes. Woodpeckers fly from tree to tree in search of insects which make up their diet. Flycatchers perch quietly, then dart out to snatch flying insects.

To escape predators, birds must be sure that their feathers are in top condition. Feathers also help a bird to maintain proper body temperature, so birds must spend time during the day grooming themselves (preening),

3

straightening the feathers, and making them waterproof with oil from a small gland at the base of the tail. Feathers are also molted, or shed, once or twice a year and replaced.

Another important behavior is communication. Birds communicate with one another in order to attract a mate, warn of a predator, or define a home territory. A territory is the area in which a bird lives. It provides cover appropriate to the species, food resources, and nesting areas. By warning others of its kind of the boundaries through song and calls, a bird protects these resources to ensure its own survival.

Birds may also use "displays", a type of visual communication. These can be as simple as puffing up the feathers on the head in warning, or as elaborate as "dances" to attract a mate. Sometimes visual clues will warn another intruding bird from the territory without the need for fighting.

A great amount of energy is spent in rearing young. First, a mate must be attracted and pairs formed between males and females. A nest site must be selected, and in some cases, an elaborate nest is constructed. Eggs must be produced and protected, and the young must be fed and reared.

All these activities comprise a bird's behavior, necessary to its own survival and that of its species.

Habitats

The place where a bird lives is called its habitat. Special adaptations allow each species to live successfully in a particular habitat. For example, in coastal areas, pelicans exist where they can survive by fishing. Other birds requiring fish in their diet live in coastal areas as well.

The wading birds, such as egrets and herons, often prefer to be inland and wade in the shallow waters of Belize's lagoons and swamps. Crooked Tree is a good example of such a place, and Jabiru storks in particular, seem to find this area hospitable to their unique way of life.

4

Belize's grasslands and savannas are home to many finches that are especially adapted to eating the seeds provided by the grasses growing there. Put these birds in a forest and they would be at a loss because proper food would not be available to them. Their adaptations allow them to live successfully only in our savannas and similar grasslands.

In the lowland tropical forests of Belize, there is an astonishing diversity of birds. Because this environment is filled with many varieties of trees and other plants, there are many food resources to support the variety of birds and other animals making their homes there. Tropical forests are considered to be among the most rich and complex habitats in the world and support a great variety and number of bird species. But it is delicately balanced and with too much disturbance by humans, it will eventually collapse.

Some birds can survive well around human habitats. In Belize's villages, grackles or "blackbirds" are often found. Vultures help with garbage clean up. Gray-breasted Martins often build their nests under the eaves of houses. And hummingbirds visit our gardens for the variety of blossoming plants found there.

Farms and ranches can be good places to spot birds of prey, called "raptors". Often the open areas associated with ranches and farms are hospitable to raptors because they can search more easily for prey in the open spaces.

A bird's special adaptations are suited to the environment, or habitat, in which it lives.

5

Bird Nests

All birds lay eggs and most incubate them by warming them with their body heat. Most birds use a nest for the early rearing of young. Nests are found in all sorts of places—on the ground, in trees, in burrows or between rocks. Nests can be elaborate or simple. A few birds are capable of moving eggs if the nest is disturbed. An example is the Pauraque, or "Who-you"—it simply lays two eggs on the ground and pushes them to another location, using its feet, if threatened. Some birds prefer their nests to be one of many in colonies with the same or mixed species. Nesting in large groups may offer a measure of safety from predators and allow them to share information on ephemeral food resources such as schools of fish.

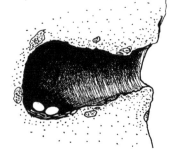

The most important functions of a nest are to offer protection for the eggs and young birds both from predators and bad weather. And, there are many types of nests. Just as birds have different physical adaptations according to the life they lead, they also have a great variety of nests. A nest can be a shallow cup of woven grasses or an elaborately woven basket. It can be made of mud or built from sticks. Or it can be at the end of a burrow dug into a bank.

If you find a nest, it can be a great opportunity to observe birds raising their young. But do so from a safe distance, using binoculars if you have them, and do not disturb the birds in any way. Sit quietly and let them go on about the important business of raising a family. And if you should find a young bird, please leave it alone. People often assume because a baby bird is on the ground or by itself, it has been abandoned. But 99% of the time the parents are close by, providing for and protecting the youngster as it learns how to be on their own. Don't keep young birds from their parents!

Bird Clocks and Calendars

Most living things, including ourselves, have a pattern of activity: a time to eat, a time to sleep, a time to work and a time to rest. Birds too, follow patterns of activity. Normally they are most active in the mornings while searching for food and singing or calling. During the middle of the day, when it is hot, they are usually much quieter. Then toward evening, they may feed again. Some birds' activities are reversed so that they are active at night, such as owls and pauraques.

Activities can change with the season. Birds' breeding cycles are often connected with the time of the year. Many birds time the raising of their young with the end of the dry season. An abundance of food is available then as trees flower and bear fruit and insect activity is at its peak. Some birds breed and raise young more than once during the year.

Migration

About 20%, or more than 100 of the birds found in Belize are migrants, that is, birds that travel from one place to another seasonally. These distances can be as great as from the Arctic to South America or as short as from the bottom of a valley to the top of a mountain. Belize is a very important wintering ground for many North American migrants. Or, looked at another way, many of Belize's birds fly north to raise their young and then return home. Some birds like the South American Swallow-tailed Kite come to Belize to breed and then return south.

There are a several theories about why birds migrate. One reason may be to take advantage of more abundant resources. Those that travel to the north will find plenty of food resources as insects emerge and fruits ripen after a cold inhospitable winter changes to spring and finally summer. There may also be less competition for suitable nesting sites and fewer predators on eggs and nestlings.

The advantages of migrating must greatly outweigh the disadvantages of staying behind. Think for a moment of some of the

7

risks: bad weather, predators, and the energy involved in flying so long and hard over such a great distance. Imagine flying over the open water of the Gulf of Mexico with no stops. Many birds do until they can rest and refuel in places like Belize's cayes before moving on even further. Many travel at night navigating by the stars and making use of generations of instinct inherited from their ancestors.

Migration and other bird behaviours are fascinating subjects that have only been touched upon here. Many books and articles have been written about birds. Many books and articles have been written on the subject; if you are interested in more information, see the Bibliography or go on-line.

Values of Birds

Birds have always been important to people. Their meat and eggs provide protein, and birds were prime prey for hunters. People discovered that birds like chickens, turkeys and quail could be domesticated so a ready food resource was then always available. Birds have figured in folklore and mythologies throughout history. For example, large raptors or birds of prey came to symbolize strength and power while owls have often stood for wisdom.

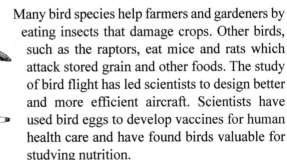

Bird products have been useful for millennia. Feathers are prized for the warmth they provide in clothing, the comfort they offer in pillows, and for their beauty. The Maya especially valued macaw feathers. In some parts of the world bird droppings, also called guano, are collected and used as a high-quality fertilizer. Peru and Chile have mined guano collected from sea-bird colonies since 1850.

Many bird species help farmers and gardeners by eating insects that damage crops. Other birds, such as the raptors, eat mice and rats which attack stored grain and other foods. The study of bird flight has led scientists to design better and more efficient aircraft. Scientists have used bird eggs to develop vaccines for human health care and have found birds valuable for studying nutrition.

Birds help us assess the health of our environment because they are highly sensitive to pollution and chemical contamination. If wild birds die or show signs of illness, it is a warning to us to clean up before other living things (including ourselves) suffer.

Birds have an important role in keeping the natural system in balance. They scatter seeds and pollinate trees, many of which provide fruits which we enjoy. They feed on insects. The presence of birds tells us that a natural system is healthy. Without birds an ecosystem would become unbalanced.

Birds add beauty in our lives and entertain us. People the world over enjoy a hobby called birdwatching, or simply, birding. More than 550 species of birds are found in Belize, so birdwatchers from other countries are eager to visit here on special birdwatching and nature tours, thus helping Belize's economy and providing jobs.

Bird Conservation

We live on a crowded planet, and every day the strain on natural systems becomes more obvious as more and more people compete for resources like fuel, wood, and food. Over the centuries human activity has caused the extinction of many organisms including more then 80 different bird species. Extinct species are gone from earth forever. Today many other species of birds are threatened with extinction because of human activities.

In many cases birds are being over-hunted, and the forests where they live are being cut to make way for milpas and pastures. Most kinds of birds cannot adjust to such drastic changes. Clearing forests affects migrant species as well. On their twice annual migrations, which are sometimes very long, they need stopping points that offer cover, food, and water.

9

The word "conservation" means the preservation of natural resources and living organisms, including birds. How does one practice conservation? Conservation becomes a grassroots effort when people see that an ecosystem or habitat is being destroyed or degraded. They speak up to those causing the destruction and correct their own behavior. Conservation movements have always been filled with people who have spoken up and made a difference.

Preservation of our natural systems and the wise use of our resources enable birds and people to coexist. We can help birds by properly disposing of litter and harmful chemicals, and by curbing pollution of their habitats. The same actions also help people. Dogs and cats left to fend for themselves can seriously harm birds by hunting them, their eggs and young. This is why pets should not be allowed to run wild; if they are well fed and cared for they have no need to hunt birds.

Wild birds usually do not make good pets; the stress of captivity often leads to disease and an early death. Instead of taking birds as pets, you can plant trees, shrubs, and other leafy cover for them. Besides beautifying your home, you'll create habitat for birds and will be able to enjoy them without putting them in a cage. Encourage your neighbors to do the same. Help birds by properly disposing of litter and other garbage so it doesn't pollute their habitats. Become involved in Belize Audubon Society or another conservation organization, either locally or internationally. Their efforts are helping not only birds but many other creatures as well.

Bird Study

Birdwatching is a rewarding hobby. It does not take sophisticated or costly equipment, although a pair of binoculars is helpful. Birds are just about everywhere. You can sit at home, or take a stroll down a road or a path into the forest or along a shoreline and you'll see many species of birds.

A good time to go birding is early in the morning, when birds are active and moving about. If you are quiet, you won't frighten them away, and you will see more.

10

Take along a notebook and pencil to jot down special features, or "field marks", of the birds you see. A field mark is a distinguishing characteristic. For example, the white eye in the White-eyed Vireo or the yellow head in the Yellow-headed Parrot.

It is also helpful to know something about how to describe a bird. Instead of saying that the bird has red in that area between the beak and the eye, you can use the proper term and say that the bird has red "lores." Not only is this more exacting, other birders and ornithologists know exactly what you are talking about.

Field marks, color pattern and other physical characteristics, along with song and behavior will help you to make a positive identification. A specialized vocabulary is used to describe unique features on birds such as "malar stripes" or "crown color." Later you can look up more information about the bird. (*see illustration below*)

Serious birders often consult more than one field guide and read the species descriptions carefully. There are several field guides available for this region as well as a guide specifically for Belize to help in

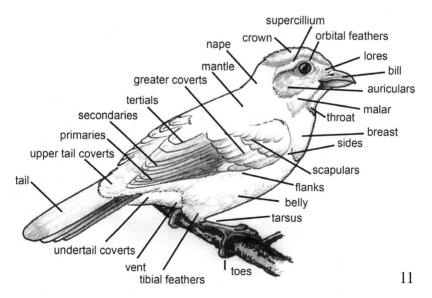

identification. These books often describe the habitats where each species is to be found and details about their life history. Such clues are also helpful in making a positive identification.

Make sure to note where you have seen the bird and what it is doing. If you have seen an interesting species along the coast for example, and later read that it is confined to higher elevations, this is a good indication that you were mistaken in your identification.

Your field notes can be valuable in locating and identifying species in Belize. Take a friend with you on your outings for fun and an extra pair of eyes to give a second opinion. Keep in mind some species—especially the flycatchers—may look very similar and require some detailed study. Report any new or unusual sightings to the Belize Audubon Society. With the wealth of habitats in our country, there is always the chance of finding something unusual or interesting.

Birds in Our Country

Geography and Habitats

Belize is not a large country, but with its coasts, cayes, and inland forests, it is blessed with a variety of habitats that offer homes to many kinds of birds. Here are a few categories of habitat; remember that different species can be found in each type.

Belize's still extensive <u>northern hardwood forests</u> are classified as "subtropical moist forests" and are a very rich and important habitat. Rainfall is between 60 and 80 inches annually. These forests grow in limestone soils and contain a wide variety of broad-leafed trees such as mahogany, sapote, and ramón.

<u>Bajo forests</u> are scattered throughout the north. These marshy areas consist of short, thin trees that exist in standing water much of the year. Orchids, bromeliads and other epiphytes—plants that usually live on other plants—are a common feature of this habitat.

<u>Southern hardwood forests</u> receive more rain than those in the north, about 80 to 100 inches annually. This area includes Belize's Maya Mountains with peaks that reach nearly 4,000 feet. Broad-leafed trees

also grow here and include quamwood, negrito, and santa maría. In the southern part of the Toledo District, which receives even more rain, trees like the cotton tree or ceiba grow to impressive heights.

When an area has been cleared for agriculture or pastures and is allowed to regenerate, the result is second growth, also called huamil (or wamil). It is characterized by fast-growing plants and trees such as the cecropia and trumpet trees, which require lots of direct sunlight. Unfortunately, this type of habitat is on the increase in Belize as more and more lands are cleared, worked, and then abandoned. Fortunately, birds are important seed dispersers and thus help regenerate growth in cleared areas.

Freshwater or riverine habitats include the forests that grow along streams, rivers and lagoons. These are highly attractive to birds and other animals and also help prevent erosion and the silting of Belize's rivers.

The Mountain Pine Ridge in the south, lies upon granite soils rather than limestone. Here we find Belize's pine forests plus oaks, grasses and shrubs and a very different assortment of birds.

Coastal savannahs are grassy, often marshy areas with short trees. Pine trees and palms are often found in this habitat. Seed-eating birds are common with the grasses serving as a major food resource.

Coastal areas are also important habitats. They include mangroves which buffer the mainland and islands against storms and keep them from eroding into the sea. Mangroves are important "reef nurseries" for marine life and the birds that feed on these resources.

Belize's cayes are small island habitats. In addition to their own unique set of birds, they are important as stop-over points for migrant species. Ambergris Caye is so close to the Yucatán Peninsula that in some ways it has more in common with the mainland than with other "true" cayes.

These categories of habitat are very general. A tropical botanist would tell you that each kind of forest includes a great variety of smaller habitats or microhabitats. One example would be a stand of cohune trees or "cohune ridge" within the greater forest. The variety of birds also changes from one microhabitat to another.

Belize's weather, including its northers and hurricanes, has played an important part in creating the habitats that give Belizean wildlife its unique character. If we allow these habitats to be cleared, Belize's bird life will be dramatically reduced.

Number of Species

By one recent count, more than 600 species of bird have been identified in Belize. Some earlier checklists have a higher count but include questionable identifications. Thus it is very important to identify a bird correctly. Note their appearance, behavior, and where you saw it. Bring a friend along to help identify it. Take pictures if possible. With proper documentation, you may be able to identify a species new to Belize. Although the country has been fairly well studied by ornithologists, it is always possible that a storm or weather front may bring in new species. A current checklist is provided toward the end of this book.

Rare and Endangered Species

"Endangered" means threatened with extinction. Put another way, it means that outside pressures are so great on a species that it may no longer be able to survive, that it may die out and no longer exist on earth.

There are many causes of bird extinction. One major cause is loss of habitat. When forests are cut and replaced by second growth, the forest dwellers lose their homes. They are forced to find other forests or die. Their special adaptations will not allow them to adjust to a cleared area. The same is true of birds that live in mangroves, for example, or in any of the other specialized habitats found in Belize.

Another cause of extinction is over-hunting. For example, in the United States the once plentiful Passenger Pigeon was wiped out by 1894. Here in Belize, the Scarlet Macaw is in similar danger. At one time macaws were fairly widespread throughout Belize; now only a few are found in the rough country of the Chiquibul. Today they are considered "rare"; tomorrow they could be gone. Other parrots are heavily hunted for pets as well. Ducks, quam, curassow, turkeys...all of these suffer from hunting pressure.

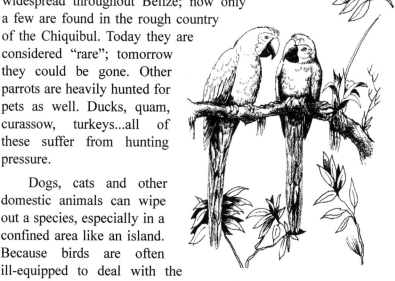

Dogs, cats and other domestic animals can wipe out a species, especially in a confined area like an island. Because birds are often ill-equipped to deal with the hunting pressure created by pets, you can help by making sure dogs and cats are well fed and kept at home so they do not need to hunt to survive.

Laws Protecting Birds

Did you know that only a few birds can be legally hunted? Birds fall under the Wildlife Protection Act of 1981, along with all wildlife found in Belize. This Act provides "for the conservation, restoration and development of wildlife, for the regulation of their use and for all other matters connected therewith."

The Act states that hunting is permitted for only six species: the Chachalaca, Crested Guan (quam), Great Curassow, Black-throated Bobwhite, the Blue-winged Teal (duck), and the Lesser Scaup. All other birds are protected and cannot legally be hunted or harassed in any way.

In addition to laws protecting species, Belize also has protected habitats. Protected habitats are in the form of national parks and nature reserves, private reserves and forest reserves. Such areas are necessary to the myriad species adapted to specialized habitats for their survival.

Further legislation concerning wildlife and protected areas is being developed. Please respect the laws that aim to protect Belize's valuable natural resources.

Belize's Protected Areas Map

Approximately 40% of Belize falls under some form of protection. Belize Audubon Society is charged with the management of nine of these protected areas.* Such areas protect valuable natural resources, watersheds and critical habitats. Many also offer unique opportunities for birdwatching and wildlife viewing. The map shows the protected areas in Belize as of 2005.

Archaeological Reserves:
15 Altun Ha
34 Cahal Pech
54 Caracol
39 Caves Branch
3   Cerros Maya
25 El Pilar
13 Lamanai
72 Lubaantun
76 Nim Li Punit
2   Santa Rita
33 Xunantunich

Bird Sanctuaries:
32 Bird Caye
5   Doubloon Bank
10 Little Guana Caye
11 Los Salones
60 Man of War Caye
69 Monkey Caye
31 Un-Named Caye

Forest Reserves:
16 Caye Caulker
55 Chiquibul
63 Columbia River
65 Deep River
9   Fresh Water Creek
50 Grants Works
75 Machaca
42 Manatee
59 Mango Creek (1)
67 Mango Creek (4)
58 Maya Mountain
68 Monkey Caye
46 Mountain Pine Ridge

47 Sibun
48 Sittee River
67 Swasey Bladen
45 Vaca

Marine Reserves:
6   Bacalar Chico
17 Caye Caulker
71 Gladden Spit and Silk Cayes
62 Glovers Reef
12 Hol Chan
79 Port Honduras
80 Sapodilla Cayes
61 Southwater Caye

National Parks:
18 Aguas Turbias
7   Bacalar Chico
49 Billy Barquedier
53 Chiquibul
41 Five Blues Lake
52 Gra Gra Lagoon
27 Guanacaste*
8   Honey Camp
70 Laughing Bird Caye
51 Mayflower Bocawina
29 Monkey Bay
35 Nojkaaxmeen Eligio Panti
78 Paynes Creek
73 Rio Blanco
81 Sarstoon-Temash
40 St. Hermans Blue Hole*

Natural Monuments:
36 Actun Tunichil Muknal*
24 Blue Hole*
44 Half Moon Caye*
38 Thousand Foot Falls
56 Victoria Peak*

Nature Reserves:
64 Bladen
22 Burdon Canal
37 Tapir Mountain*

Private Reserves (Official):
21 Community Baboon Sanctuary
77 Golden Stream
28 Monkey Bay
19 Rio Bravo

Private Reserves (Unofficial):
26 Aguacate Lagoon
30 Runaway Creek
4   Shipstern

Wildlife Sanctuaries:
74 Aguacaliente
57 Cockscomb Basin*
1   Corozal Bay
14 Crooked Tree*
43 Gales Point
20 Spanish Creek
23 Swallow Caye

16

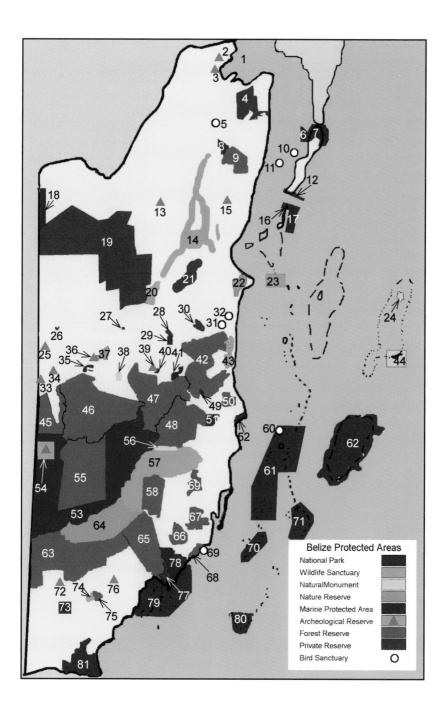

Belize Protected Areas

National Park	
Wildlife Sanctuary	
NaturalMonument	
Nature Reserve	
Marine Protected Area	
Archeological Reserve	▲
Forest Reserve	
Private Reserve	
Bird Sanctuary	○

101 Birds of Belize
Species Accounts

Y̶ou may wonder why the following birds were selected from the more than 550 found in the country. It wasn't easy! The idea was to highlight some of Belize's more commonly found birds, those that people can see with just a little effort in the appropriate habitats, or those they see everyday and may have wondered about.

A few of Belize's especially interesting or beautiful birds are also included, as well as several with special conservation concerns. It is hoped that interest in birds will be promoted here so that the reader is encouraged to become active in one of Belize's conservation organizations and practice conservation at an individual level.

Birds of Belize by H. Lee Jones includes all the birds found in Belize, including the migrants. Field guides for Belize, Mexico and Central America provide additional information and illustrations for comparison. A North American field guide is a useful supplement for the migrant species.

You may also be wondering why the birds are listed in the following order. This type of classification follows an ascending order of what scientists currently regard as the most primitive species first to those most highly evolved.

Great Tinamou

Tinamus major

Other Names: Tinamú Grande, Nom, Ix Mancolol, Partridge

These ground dwelling birds live in Belize's still extensive northern and southern hardwood forests where they are fairly common. Rarely will a tinamou fly if disturbed, preferring instead to scurry into the dense undergrowth of the forest floor when threatened.

The Great Tinamou is the largest of Belize's four species, about 15 inches from head to tail. The dark body blends into the forest which helps to protect the bird against predators. Tinamous have solitary habits and spend their days foraging for seeds and insects on the ground. They are not often seen, but you may hear its haunting, drawn out whistle, particularly at twilight.

Like all tinamous, the Great Tinamou lays its eggs on the forest floor, often at the base of a tree or between buttressed roots. The three to five glossy turquoise eggs are usually well concealed by leaf litter. The male assumes care of the young after hatching.

Black-bellied Whistling Duck
Dendrocygna autumnalis
Other Names: Pato Pijiji Aliblanco,
Tree Duck

This beautiful duck has a high-pitched, piping call which gives it its name. With its long neck and large body, it looks a bit like a goose. In flight, large, white wing patches stand out making it easily recognizable. Unlike most ducks, Whistling Ducks often perch high in trees and are often known as "tree ducks."

The whistling duck dives and swims well but often feeds in shallow water on leaves, shoots, seeds, and insects. A social bird, it is often found in small flocks. Its preferred habitat is tree-lined ponds or freshwater lagoons, and it nests in tree cavities as high as 30 feet above the ground. Like most ducks, it normally lays a large clutch of eggs since the loss of young to predators is high. When hatched, the young ducks jump from their nest to the ground to take to the water with their parents—quite an amazing leap for ducklings too young to fly.

Blue-winged Teal
Anas discors

Other Names: Cerceta Aliazul Clara, Cutz-Ha

This small migratory duck is seen for only a few months of the year in Belize. In April and May it flies north to nest and raise its young before heading back south in September and October for the better part of the year. Some teal stop only to rest and "refuel" in Belize while others stay several weeks or months in places like Crooked Tree Wildlife Sanctuary.

Like most ducks, the Blue-winged Teal is normally seen in flocks near water. Males have a blue-gray head, and females are gray-brown; both have a small blue patch on the wing. Teals feed by tilting tails up and ducking head, neck, and breast underwater while "dabbling" with broad, flattened bills for bits of vegetation and aquatic creatures.

The teal's breeding grounds extend from Alaska and northern Canada throughout the southern United States. Years ago teal were heavily hunted in Belize at places like Cox Lagoon, and their numbers seriously declined. This is another species that deserves our protection and consideration.

Plain Chachalaca

Ortalis vetula

Other Names: Chachalaca Vetula, Ix Bach, Cockrico

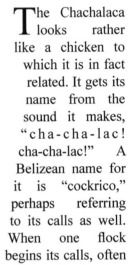

The Chachalaca looks rather like a chicken to which it is in fact related. It gets its name from the sound it makes, "cha-cha-lac! cha-cha-lac!" A Belizean name for it is "cockrico," perhaps referring to its calls as well. When one flock begins its calls, often before dawn, it usually inspires nearby flocks to answer, creating a noisy commotion.

As its name suggests, this is a rather plain bird, mostly gray-brown in color, although males have a bare red throat patch. Chachalacas are found in flocks of several individuals in thickets, dense second growth, and savannahs. With strong well-developed legs, it is equally at home on the ground or in the treetops. Principal foods are fruits and buds. Nests are made of twigs and fibrous materials a few feet to 25 feet up a tree. Two or three white, rough-shelled eggs are usual. The downy young leave the nest after hatching and can climb into the treetops where they are fed by the adults.

Crested Guan

Penelope purpurascens

Other Names: Pava Cojolita, Ah Cox, Quam

To most people in Belize, this large dark bird is known as the "quam" and is a favorite game bird. It is found in tall forests, often in the treetops. When alarmed, it calls in a high-pitched voice, making it an easy target. Over-hunting and loss of forest habitat are reducing its numbers drastically here as well as in most of Central America.

Large and heavy bodied, the quam has strong legs and toes suitable for perching and clambering among the branches. Its wings make a rhythmic noise as it flies, perhaps from the effort of propelling such a heavy body through the air. The quam's preferred foods are fruits, seeds, leaves, and insects. This shy bird is often found in pairs or in small family groups. Its nest is built 30 or more feet up in mature trees. The quam's eggs are creamy white with finely pitted shells.

Great Curassow

Crax rubra

Other Names: Hocofaisán, K'ambul, Bolonchan

An elegant bird, the handsome male is glossy black with a bright yellow unfeathered knob beneath his curling crest. The brown female is attractively striped black and white which allows her to blend in with her surroundings.

Curassows feed on fruits, seeds, and insects on the ground. Males make a low pitched booming sound which is often difficult to locate. Curassows remain faithful to one mate, and build a nest perhaps 30 or more feet up in a tree. The female lays two rough-shelled white eggs, and the chicks are downy and protectively striped. The male leads the family around by day, keeping in touch by making low pitched grunting calls. At night the hen roosts with a chick protected under each wing. Like the quam, the curassow suffers from over-hunting and loss of its forest habitat. These magnificent birds deserve our consideration and should not be hunted in excess or soon we will have none.

Ocellated Turkey

Meleagris ocellata

Other Names: Guajolote Ocelado, Kuts, Ucutz Ilchican

The Ocellated Turkey is threatened throughout its range, again due to over-hunting and loss of forests. This large turkey is called "ocellated" for the eye spots, or "ocelli," on its feathers. The male turkey has orange-red fleshy knobs on its naked blue head and spurs like a rooster. The female is less brightly marked and lacks spurs.

Turkeys are found both in groups and singly, where they feed on the ground searching for berries, nuts, seeds, and insects, which make up their diet. Nests are little more than a depression in a sheltered spot on the forest floor. Eight or more brown speckled eggs are laid. This handsome bird has been nearly wiped out in much of its range, and to date captive breeding programs have had little success. Belize is one of the last places in the world where it exists, especially northwestern Belize. In recent years, it has been nearly wiped out from the Chiquibul, a former stronghold. We need to do our best to conserve it.

Black-throated Bobwhite
Colinus nigrogularis

Other Names: Codorniz Cotuí Yucateca, Ah Cul, Bech'

Coveys or small flocks of ground-dwelling Bobwhites are found in savannahs, cleared areas, and fields. Chicken-like, they scratch at the ground searching for insects, seeds, and berries. Often they can be approached fairly closely before they explode into flight.

Bobwhites are members of the quail family and take their name from their call, a whistled "bobwhite!" Bobwhites appear to have been important to the Maya. Their bones have been found in great numbers in caches, burial chambers, and temple debris. It's not known whether they were domesticated, heavily hunted for food, or perhaps had some ceremonial significance.

Male birds have a black head and throat while females are brown in the same areas. Nests are made of grass in a hollowed area on the ground.

Pied-billed Grebe
Podilymbus podiceps

Other Names: Zambullidor Piquigrueso, Ah Bich

L ooking out onto a lagoon or quiet aguada in Belize, you may see small, dark birds paddling peacefully on the surface or occasionally diving underwater. Commonly mistaken as ducks, these small aquatic birds are not ducks at all but grebes. They can be distinguished at a glance by their small slender bills. In Belize, two species are found, the Pied-billed and the Least Grebe.

The Pied-billed Grebe is fairly common in Belize from about October to mid-March. During these months, its throat is white; during the breeding season in North America the throat becomes black. The grebe's special distinction is its bill; normally light-colored and plain, it sports a black band during breeding season.

The grebe is not an especially good flier but is very much at home in the water, seldom coming ashore, and is quite good at swimming underwater after small fish or aquatic insects. Grebes prefer marshy areas for nesting and build floating raft-like nests.

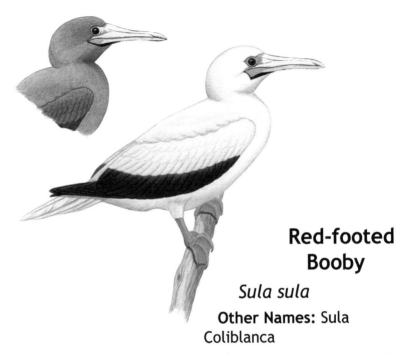

Red-footed Booby

Sula sula

Other Names: Sula Coliblanca

Situated in Lighthouse Reef, Half Moon Caye became Belize's first Natural Monument in 1982. This 45-acre caye is home to a breeding colony of approximately 4,000 Red footed Boobies as well as other marine bird species. With its red webbed feet and legs, the Half Moon Caye boobies are mainly of the white color phase. Elsewhere in the Caribbean, they are normally brown or gray. Both color phases have a white tail.

Although related to Pelicans, boobies are much smaller with narrow wings tipped in black. Red-footed Boobies are strong fliers and well adapted for soaring over open ocean and diving from great heights for fish or squid. Unlike other boobies which simply lay their eggs on the ground, Red-footed Boobies nest in mangroves or low bushes.

Because of their isolated existence on remote cayes, boobies had no reason to develop a fear of man. Sailors christened them "boobies" because when hunted by men the birds were too "stupid" to run. Sailors clubbed them and threw their carcasses into the "booby hatch" where the ship's fresh meat was kept.

Brown Pelican
Pelecanus occidentalis

Other Names: Pelícano Pardo

A large bulky body, short stubby legs and long bill makes the Brown Pelican appear anything but beautiful, but a wingspan of nearly seven and a half feet makes this awkward-looking bird a graceful flier, gliding on air currents along the coasts.

With daring aerial dives into schools of surface-feeding fish, the pelican scoops fish into its bill, which has an expandable pouch. Any water that is scooped up is filtered out over the bill's edges and the pelican has its meal, ready to be eaten or temporarily stored. The Brown Pelican is a familiar sight along Belize City's shores where it roosts on piers or pilings. It can be seen performing its spectacular fishing feats or just floating with wings loosely folded over its back.

Brown Pelicans prefer a saltwater environment and are only rarely found inland. Pelicans nest in colonies and use loosely constructed nests in low bushes or sometimes on the ground, where they lay two or three white eggs. Immature birds are grayish-brown and develop the white head and neck plumage of the adult by the third year.

Neotropic Cormorant
Phalacrocorax brasilianus

Other Names: Cormorán, Sheg

A long Belize's rivers and lagoons, a slender dark head pokes up from the water. Before you are quite sure that you have seen it, the Neotropic Cormorant dives out of sight. With its heavy body, the cormorant seems better suited for diving than flying, but if disturbed it runs along the water's surface gaining momentum for flight. It is often seen in small groups perched on logs with wings outspread, all the better for the sun to dry them.

The term "olivaceous" is used to describe its greenish-brown color, but when wet, this bird appears dark brown or black. It has a long hooked bill distinctive of its type, and a dark yellow throat pouch. It is somewhat smaller than the Double-crested Cormorant which is more often found along Belize's coasts. A colonial breeder, the Neotropic Cormorant often gathers at the Crooked Tree Wildlife Sanctuary in large numbers. Belizeans know it as "sheg."

Anhinga

Anhinga anhinga

Other Names: Anhinga Americana, Darter, Snake Bird

Sometimes called the "snake bird" for its long S-shaped neck, the anhinga can be distinguished from cormorants by its lighter brown color and because it is much thinner. It prefers the same river and lagoon habitats as the Neotropic Cormorant. Its webbed feet allow it to swim swiftly underwater after fish which it spears with its long pointed bill. Besides being well adapted to swimming and diving, anhingas are also good fliers, moving with deep, powerful wing beats.

Because anhingas lack the waterproofing oil for their feathers which most aquatic birds possess, they often spread their wings to dry them in the sun. Male anhingas have white plumes along their wings and back while females have a buff-brown head and neck.

Also known as "darters," anhingas nest in colonies. They build a small stick platform in trees, and a pair normally produces three to five blue eggs with a chalky white coating.

31

Magnificent Frigatebird

Fregata magnificens

Other Names: Fragata Pelágica, Man-o-War

S eafarers named this graceful flier after the frigate, a swift warship. Along this same theme, Belizeans know it as "man-o-war." In fact, there is a bird sanctuary on Man of War Caye. Common along Belize's coasts and cayes, this large bird has a wingspan of nearly eight feet enabling it to sail over vast expanses of ocean in search of food. Frigatebirds snatch fish from the water's surface or pirate them from other birds in daring aerial acrobatics.

Basically black, the male Man-o-War becomes truly magnificent during courtship, inflating his red throat pouch to impress the opposite sex. Females are white-throated with no pouch. Because Frigate birds spend much of their life in flight, their small, weak feet are used mainly to perch at their breeding grounds. They nest in colonies, building a stick platform in small trees or shrubs or on the ground. A pair usually produces a single white egg.

Great Blue Heron
Ardea herodias

Other Names: Garzón Cenizo, Full-pot

This bird, which stands about four feet tall, belongs in the heron family which must have wetlands to survive. Its long dark legs are perfectly adapted to wading in shallow waters and marshy lagoons. Here it stands motionlessly, poised for the moment when a fish or other prey swims past. Then it strikes with lightning speed.

Normally found alone, the Great Blue flies with its head pulled back and with long slow wing beats. As its name suggests, this bird has a gray-blue body, with attractive striping on its head and neck and short gray plumes extending from the back of its head. Because of its large size, it is not easily mistaken for any other species. There is however, a morph, or variation, of the species which is white and not often seen here.

In Belize, the Great Blue Heron is sometimes called "full-pot," and has been hunted heavily in some places. Because wetland areas are disappearing throughout its range, this bird deserves protection here in Belize where it still has a home.

33

Great Egret

Ardea alba

Other Names: Garzón Blanco, Bach Ha, Gaulin

L ike the Great Blue Heron, the Great Egret prefers the shallow waters of Belize's wetlands. It is an entirely different species from the Great Blue Heron, although both are in the same family and are sometimes seen together. The Great Egret is also a bit smaller and is sighted more frequently. Belizeans often refer to this, and other herons, as "Gaulin."

This large, white bird is often poised motionlessly along Belize's roads and highways where there is standing water. Like most herons, it is not noted for its song, producing only a harsh squawking sound. During the breeding season, the Great Egret develops long delicate plumes. These are so lovely that in the early 1900's, egret plumes, or "aigrettes," were in great demand for ladies' fashions, and heavy hunting nearly wiped the birds out. Fortunately, they have been allowed to recover.

Cattle Egret
Bubulcus ibis

Other Names: Garza Ganadera

In many villages in Belize, this small white egret is a common sight following grazing cattle or horses. Unlike most other egrets, the Cattle Egret prefers to forage on land eating insects, especially grasshoppers that large grazing animals have disturbed. It is most often seen in small groups, but at night, large flocks of these birds converge on a favorite roosting place.

Normally all white, this small egret develops buff plumage on its head, back, and breast and a bright orange bill during the breeding season. It builds stick nests in dense tree-top colonies.

The Cattle Egret is a native of Africa, but sometime in the 1880's it crossed the Atlantic Ocean and arrived in South America. From there, it has steadily moved north.

Agami Heron

Agamia agami

Other Names: Garza Estilet, Blue Jacket

The Agami Heron is surely one of the most beautiful herons in the world, but it is secretive and seldom seen. Agamis are usually found alone except in the breeding season when they may be seen in pairs. The Agami is considered rare in Belize, but its shy habits may make it seem more scarce than it really is.

This heron prefers large secluded marshy areas or quiet inland woodside streams. It wades in shallow water searching for frogs and fishes with its very long bill. If disturbed, it immediately takes cover. The Agami is mainly warm brown in color, with green wings. During the breeding season it develops silver-blue nuptial plumes which trail down from the head and back. Facial skin on the males becomes reddish and on females, greenish. Perhaps this is where it gets its Belizean name, "blue jacket."

For nesting, an Agami builds a rounded platform from small twigs, often in the company of other herons, and lays two and sometimes three blue-green eggs.

Boat-billed Heron
Cochlearius cochlearius
Other Names: Garza Cucharón, Kuka', Cooper

This unusual member of the heron family has an especially distinctive large, wide bill. Nobody knows why the bill is so large. It may be especially adapted for "scooping" food items from the aquatic habitat where it lives, or it may be used in courtship displays. Whatever the case, its bill is very different from the thin, sharp bills of other heron species. This heron is found along river banks, swamps and ponds, and in mangrove areas.

The Boat-bill is nocturnal and has the large eyes typical of birds and other animals that are active at night. Like most other herons, the Boat-billed Heron prefers the company of other members of its own species. During the day it roosts in groups of up to 50 birds, often with much loud squawking. These birds build stick nests, often overhanging the water, and lay two to three eggs. A Belizean name for this heron is "cooper."

Roseate Spoonbill
Ajaia ajaja

Other Names: Ibis Espátula

Another bird that lives in Belize's fresh and saltwater wetlands is the Roseate Spoonbill. Easily distinguished by its pink color, it has a long flattened "spoonbill" especially adapted to its feeding habits. Wading in shallow water, the bird searches for shrimp and small fish by swinging its slightly opened bill from side to side, then snapping it shut around its prey.

Because of its attractive pink color, this bird was once hunted for its plumes, but the species has slowly recovered. During the breeding season the facial skin turns orangish and the

throat area becomes bluish-green. The Roseate Spoonbill nests in dense mangroves, shrubs, or low-growing trees in colonies, often with heron species. It usually produces two to four white eggs blotched with brown in a well constructed cup nest of sticks. Young birds are a pale pink and have a feathered rather than a bald head; it takes them three years to obtain adult plumage.

Jabiru

Jabiru mycteria

Other Names: Cigueña Jabirú, Fillymingo, Turk

Belizeans can be especially proud that for at least part of the year the majestic Jabiru stork makes its home in our marshy savannahs. Here it is often known as "fillymingo" or "turk." Standing nearly five feet tall with an eight-foot wingspan, it is the largest stork in the New World. Its large, heavy bill is nearly 12 inches long and is well suited for catching frogs, fish, and snakes, all preferred food items. The collar around the neck changes from red to orange depending on the bird's stress level.

It is thought that an estimated nine to twelve pairs of Jabiru storks arrive in late November or early December, probably from southern Mexico (however, new research should shed further light on this situation). Each pair builds an enormous stick nest high in a tree and then produces two to three eggs. The chicks are a sooty black, gradually turning white. At the beginning of the rainy season, as the areas they prefer become flooded, the Jabirus return to Mexico.

Wood Stork

Mycteria americana

Other Names: Cigueña Americana, John Crow Culu

The Wood Stork, sometimes known as "John Crow Culu" in Belize, makes its home in freshwater or coastal swamps, wading up to its belly on long legs. Although it has a white body like many other large wading birds, its grayish-black naked head and down-turned bill make it easy to recognize. Often several birds move through shallow water in formation, working together to herd and concentrate fish which they snap up in their bills.

Wood Storks roost in dense colonies in mangroves and other vegetation, building platform nests of sticks and leafy twigs. Many people in Belize enjoy barbecuing this bird's meat—even though it is illegal—and over the years its numbers have been greatly reduced. In other parts of the world, habitat loss is a major problem. Shipstern Nature Reserve in northern Belize has a program to protect the Wood Stork colonies while the young are being raised. Its populations are slowly recovering thanks to protection from wardens based at a camp near the colony. The colony has now expanded to two other cayes with breeding pairs numbering perhaps more than 300.

Black Vulture

Coragyps atratus

Other Names: Carroñero Común, Ch'om, John Crow

Called "John Crow" in Belize, the Black Vulture is a familiar sight over almost every part of our country except the cayes. Often seen in flocks gliding on thermals in the open skies, the Black Vulture has a dark naked head and white patches at the tips of its wings. This is how you can distinguish it from the red-headed Turkey Vulture which is sometimes seen with it.

Vultures perform a valuable service to us, scavenging garbage and refuse around many villages. Their main source of food is carrion, or dead animals, though they will occasionally eat fruit. The vulture's naked head evolved in response to its habit of thrusting it into spoiling carcasses. Vultures travel in flocks, and there is much pushing and shoving when they discover a carcass. Black Vultures lay two whitish splotched eggs on the ground, in caves, crevices, or occasionally tree stumps. Both parents incubate the eggs and regurgitate food to the young.

King Vulture
Sarcoramphus papa

Other Names: Carroñero Rey, Zopiloto Rey, Oc, King John Crow

Occasionally, if you are watching a group of vultures soaring high overhead, you may notice an even larger white bird with black edged wings. If you are lucky, you might be able to see its naked head marked in orange, yellow, bright red, and blue.

Like other vultures, the King feeds on dead animals. When it arrives at a spoiling carcass, other vulture species make way for the King. It can be found gliding over Belize's forests and in the Mountain Pine Ridge. Although the sense of smell in birds is normally not well developed, King Vultures can locate spoiling carcasses by smell. Not a great deal is known about its nesting habits. Usually one chick is hatched, and it remains black for three or four years before slowly gaining the adult's white feathers. Because forest lands are shrinking throughout Mexico and Central America, this bird is becoming scarce. Where Belize has forests, there are still healthy populations.

White-tailed Kite
Elanus leucurus

Other Names: Milano Coliblanco, Ah Chuy

In open country and agricultural areas, this sleek bird is a familiar sight as it sails gracefully overhead. Frequently, in a feat that uses a tremendous amount of energy, it hovers in mid-air as it scans the ground for the rodents or large grasshoppers that make up its diet.

This kite is a raptor, or bird of prey, having talons and a bill adapted to holding and tearing its kill. Raptors have excellent vision and can see their prey from great heights and long distances. In the air, the kite can be distinguished from other raptors by its long, pointed wings and white underparts. Many people think that raptors take their chickens. In reality, most raptors like the Black-shouldered Kite perform a valuable service by keeping pest populations down.

Most often, this kite nests high in a solitary tree where it builds a cup nest of twigs and lines it with finer material. The female lays three to five white eggs marked with brown.

43

Snail Kite
Rostrhamus sociabilis
Other Names: Milano Caracolero

The Snail Kite is always found in wetland areas where its only food is a large snail called the "apple snail." This raptor soars slowly over the water looking for apple snails and plucks them up with its feet. Then it returns to a perch where it pulls the snail from its shell with a long, thin, hooked beak. Without wetland areas and the apple snail it relies on, this kite cannot survive.

Snail Kites are sexually dimorphic; that is, males and females look different. The male bird is a slaty black with a reddish eye, while the female is a mottled brown and a bit larger in size. At Crooked Tree Wildlife Sanctuary, Snail Kites were seen for the first time stealing apple snails from limpkins, a large wading bird, rather than always hunting snails for themselves. This act of piracy is called "kleptoparasitism."

Black-collared Hawk
Busarellus nigricollis

Other Names: Gavilán Conchero, Chestnut Hawk, Fishing Hawk

This large handsome hawk, sometimes called "chestnut hawk" or "fishing hawk," prefers to live near water. It also likes forested areas, so the swampy areas and lagoons in Belize's northern forests make a good habitat for this fairly common resident.

As in many birds of prey, males and females look alike. The Black-collared Hawk is attractively marked, mainly reddish brown with a black collar and light head. It is fairly large, with a short tail and wings. When hunting, this hawk perches on a snag overlooking the water. When it spies prey, it swoops down and snatches it from the water's surface taking care not to get thoroughly soaked. It hunts fish, frogs, mammals, large insects, and even small birds.

The Black-collared Hawk builds a platform nest 40 to 50 feet up in a tree, and a pair usually produces one or two eggs.

White Hawk

Leucopternis albicollis

Other Names: Aguililla Blanca, Cot

This attractive hawk is unmistakable: all white with black edging on its wings and tail. Although this species is widespread, it is not often seen because it lives in densely forested areas. However, you can sometimes see it as it soars over Belize's tall forests and along their edges. It perches quietly along the forest edge where it waits for its prey: snakes and other reptiles, small mammals, insects, and even small birds.

The White Hawk is not especially shy and can sometimes be approached quite closely. Like all birds of prey, this hawk does not have a song and only utters a harsh scream. It builds a nest of twigs and sticks lined with dead leaves in tall trees, often among epiphytes. It usually produces one egg which is bluish white with brown markings. Like most raptors, the young mature and breed only after three or four years.

46

Great Black-Hawk
Buteogallus urubitinga

Other Names: Aguililla Negra

This large black hawk is commonly found along forest rivers and, occasionally, marshy savannahs. In flight it can be distinguished from other dark-colored hawks by two white bands on its tail. While perched, you may be able to see its lightly barred "trousers." Like all raptors, it is not in the least musical, but it does have a distinctive, shrill whistle.

Preferred foods include snakes, frogs, lizards, turtles, crabs, and occasionally carrion. It nests in trees, both high and low, in cupped stick nests lined with dead leaves. Normally one pale blue egg is laid which is spotted reddish brown. Until young birds obtain adult plumage, they are dark brown and spotted light brown on the head and neck with many dark brown tail bands.

Roadside Hawk

Buteo magnirostris

Other Names: Aguililla Caminera, Ch'uy, Insect Hawk

Certainly all of us have seen this familiar gray-brown hawk perched along our roads. It is probably Belize's most common bird of prey, and its numbers are increasing as forests are cut down because it is one of the few hawks which can make a living in open areas and secondary growth.

It can exist in close contact with man and is often wrongly accused of taking chickens. This isn't the case at all; this bird prefers large insects, and in fact used to be called the "Insect Hawk." Lizards, some snakes, and rodents are also part of its diet. In this way it aids man, by helping control pests. The Roadside Hawk can often be approached quite closely before giving its distinctive "kee-wah!" call and flapping off.

During the dry season, it builds a stick platform nest at medium heights in trees at woodland edges and the female lays two brown-speckled white eggs

Harpy Eagle

Harpia harpyja

Other Names: Aguila harpía

By some reckonings, this is the largest eagle in the world. With a six-foot wingspan and standing nearly three feet tall, it is a most impressive bird. Females, which are larger than males, can weigh as much as 20 pounds. They are beautifully marked with a chest band, dark slate gray upperparts and white underparts. Both male and female have the distinctive double crest which distinguishes it from other crested eagles found in Belize. This is the Harpy Eagle, a bird on the "most wanted" list by birders.

This large forest eagle mates for life and nests in high, widely spaced trees in expansive forested areas. It feeds mainly on arboreal mammals including opossums and monkeys. There are very few historical records of harpies in Belize although it is a bird that has been reported often. In recent years, a harpy was filmed in the Chiquibul near the Maya site, Caracol. Unfortunately, this bird was ultimately shot and killed. Its feet and talons were recovered from a small village near the Belize-Guatemala border. The people said they were afraid it would take their children. Although this belief is false, it caused the death of this bird.

Early success has been reported in restablishing the Harpy Eagle in Belize through an ongoing captive release program by the Belize Zoo and Tropical Education Center and Birds without Borders in cooperation with the Peregrine Fund Panama.

Ornate Hawk-Eagle
Spizaetus ornatus
Other Names: Aguila Elegante, Curassaw Hawk

Without a doubt one of the world's most beautiful eagles, this elegant bird sports a black crest and multicolored rust, brown, black, and white plumage deservingly called "ornate." It is found only in heavily forested areas, flying alone and occasionally giving voice to a high-pitched scream.

This large and powerful hawk-eagle is capable of taking mammals and large birds, and has even been known to kill an adult curassow. It is said to be known as the "curassow hawk" in some parts of Belize. Because it prefers to hunt in tall tropical forest areas, it is rarely found near villages and so is not a threat to domestic fowl. Its normal method of hunting is at medium height in the forest where it swoops down on prey which includes lizards and snakes.

The Ornate Hawk-Eagle builds a large stick nest in a tall, mature tree and hatches one downy white chick. Both parents attend the chick in the nest and continue to feed it for some time after it has fledged.

Laughing Falcon
Herpetotheres cachinnans
Other Names: Halcón Guaco, Kos

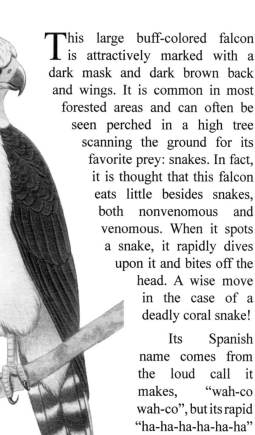

This large buff-colored falcon is attractively marked with a dark mask and dark brown back and wings. It is common in most forested areas and can often be seen perched in a high tree scanning the ground for its favorite prey: snakes. In fact, it is thought that this falcon eats little besides snakes, both nonvenomous and venomous. When it spots a snake, it rapidly dives upon it and bites off the head. A wise move in the case of a deadly coral snake!

Its Spanish name comes from the loud call it makes, "wah-co wah-co", but its rapid "ha-ha-ha-ha-ha-ha" sounds rather like crazy human laughter. During courtship, the male and female call back and forth in an unforgettable duet. During the dry season, the Laughing Falcon nests in the hollow of a large tree or a hole in a cliff, and occasionally reuses another hawk's stick nest. The single youngster is buffy colored and has a dark mask like the adults.

51

Bat Falcon

Falco rufigularis

Other Names: Halcón Enano, E'pi', Ah Chu'uy, Lion Hawk

A small but powerful bird of prey, the Bat Falcon is an expert flier. It is usually seen alone or in pairs along forest edges, clearings, second growth, or agricultural areas. With narrow pointed wings, falcons are seldom seen soaring, but instead flap rapidly and agilely in pursuit of prey. Such swift flight allows the Bat Falcon to catch small birds, insects, and at dusk, bats. Falcons are known for their spectacular dives upon prey.

As with all falcons, the female is larger than the male. Both sexes are attractively marked with rusty orange breasts and gray-blue "helmets." If they have not been harassed by people, they often will allow a close approach. During the dry season Bat Falcons nest high in a tree in holes sometimes borrowed from woodpeckers. A pair usually produces two cream-colored eggs blotched with brown. A Belizean name for this bird is "lion hawk".

Gray-necked Wood-Rail

Aramides cajanea

Other Names: Ralón Cuelligris, Ulumha, Top-na-chick

The "top na chick" is a familiar sight. Though it is a shy bird, most of us have caught a glimpse of the it near villages, usually around marshy areas and stream beds.

A member of the rail family, top-na-chick is characterized by long red legs, short rounded wings, and a short tail. Although it can fly, if frightened it tends to dash into dense undergrowth where it is rapidly lost from sight. The top-na-chick is most active at dawn and dusk, and it is at these times when one is most likely to hear its chicken-like cackle. It searches among leaves and in mud for frogs, seeds, berries, and palm fruits. A mass of dead vegetation and twigs forms the Wood-Rail's nest, which it builds six to ten feet up in a dense thicket, usually near water. The females lay three dull white eggs with brown and lilac blotches.

Sungrebe

Heliornis fulica

Other Names: Pájaro Cantil, Xpatux Já, American Finfoot

Although it swims like a duck and dives like a grebe, the Sungrebe is in its own unique family which is distantly related to the rails. Birders visiting Belize consider a look at this bird a prized sighting.

Swimming half submerged in streams and along densely vegetated banks, the Sungrebe prefers quiet waters as it searches for the fish, insects, and crustaceans which make up most of its diet. It has a boldly patterned black-and-white head and neck, and lobed toes which gave rise to its old name which was "American Finfoot". It builds stick nests above water and transports the chicks in hollows on the adult's sides. The Sungrebe can both swim and fly with its young protected in this manner until they are ready to live on their own.

Killdeer

Charadrius vociferus

Other Names: Chorlito Tildío

The name "killdeer" is similar to this species' call, and does not refer to any violence against deer. Widespread in North America, the Killdeer makes Belize a stopping off point, or, for many birds, a southern home. They are often seen in late December in northern Belize, in time for the annual Christmas Bird Counts.

A member of the Plover family, Killdeer prefer grasslands and open land. Usually found in small flocks, the Killdeer is immediately recognizable by two black bands on its throat and breast. It is long-legged and forages on the ground for insects. If frightened, the Killdeer may run and stop abruptly. When it is threatened at its nest, the Killdeer convincingly fakes a broken wing and cries pathetically while it tries to lead the predator from its nest. Its breeding grounds are throughout most of North America south of central Alaska.

Northern Jacana

Jacana spinosa

Other Names: Jacana Centroamericana, Ulumha, Lily Trotter,
Georgie Bull

A t first glance, the Jacana has absurdly long legs and feet, but its long toes aid it in walking on aquatic vegetation; in fact, it is sometimes called the "lily trotter." Here in Belize it is more commonly know as "georgie bull" and is a familiar sight along rivers and marshes.

A handsome bird with yellow wing linings and yellow face shield, the male Jacana assumes all responsibility for building a shallow nest among the floating plants. He then incubates the brown-and-black blotched eggs, usually four in number. When the young have hatched, he cares for them, sometimes sheltering the chicks under his wings during heavy rains. Meanwhile, the female defends the territory of the two to four males for which she has provided eggs. This unusual mating system is called "polyandry." Both sexes have yellow spurs on the wings that are used in displays and defensive behavior.

Spotted Sandpiper

Actitis macularia

Other Names: Playerito Alzacolita, Shaky Batty

The Spotted Sandpiper is another migrant species seen during the rainy season months. It searches for food in a variety of habitats including coastal beaches, mangrove swamps, marshy areas, and inland streams. It is usually alone and vigorously defends its territory against other Spotted Sandpipers.

"Shaky Batty" well deserves its Belizean name, for its head and tail bob in continuous motion as it pecks at insects and other invertebrates at waters' edge. The Spotted Sandpiper breeds throughout North America and develops boldly spotted underparts as part of its breeding plumage. This species was recently determined to be "polyandrous," which means the female mates with more than one male, lays several clutches of eggs, and each male incubates his clutch. It is thought that this behavior evolved as a defense against predators.

Laughing Gull

Leucophaeus atricilla

Other Names: Gaviota Risueña, Laughing Bird

This gull is found along coastal areas and mangroves. It has a dark hood and grayish wings shading to black at the tips when in its breeding plumage. During other times of the year, its hood is less distinct. As you might guess from the name, its variety of calls resemble human laughter. It is well known in Belize as "laughing bird;" in fact, Laughing Bird Caye is now a national park.

This gull flies gracefully with slow wingbeats and often soars. It prefers the company of large flocks of its own kind as well as other gulls and terns. Its diet includes scraps and carrion from fishing boats plus the fish, shrimp, and crabs it finds in shallow water. There are even accounts of Laughing Gulls landing on the heads of pelicans that have just surfaced after a dive; as the pelican swallows its catch, the gull tries to snatch it away.

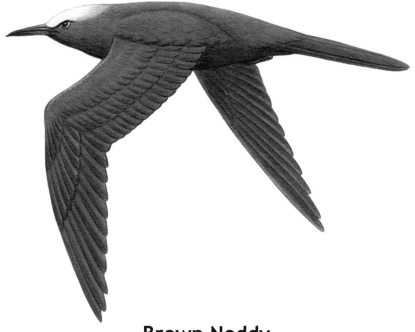

Brown Noddy

Anous stolidus

Other Names: Golondrina Marina Gorriblanca

Like most other terns, the Brown Noddy prefers marine environments and can be seen along the southern cayes. While most terns are white with dark markings, the Brown Noddy is just the reverse: brown with a white cap.

Noddies live at sea throughout the tropics and during the breeding season use sandy islands like our Glover's Reef cayes. The females lay a single egg on the ground or in low shrubs. Nests are sometimes lined with bits of coral and shells. Unfortunately the quash, or coatimundi, has been introduced to Glover's Reef and has preyed heavily upon the Noddy colony, which has no defense against this unfamiliar and expert predator. This is a good example of why wild creatures should not be moved from their native habitats. When they are, such exotics either die out or threaten other creatures naturally occurring in the area.

Bridled Tern
Onychotrian anaethetus
Other Names: Charrán Monja

Sleek and slender, the Bridled Tern is found in areas of warm seas around the world. In Belize, it lives on the southern cayes. Its long, pointed wings, deeply forked tail, and slender bill make it easy to tell from other gulls.

Terns feed by diving on fish and other surface-swimming creatures. They fly alone or in small groups with quick, steady wing beats, never soaring. For breeding plumage, this tern develops a pale gray collar while its upper parts are mainly dark. A light patch on its forehead extends behind the eye in a stripe which helps to distinguish it from other terns. The remainder of the year its plumage is similar, but with white streaks on the crown and nape. It nests in colonies on offshore islands and lays just one egg on the ground using little nesting material.

Red-billed Pigeon
Patagioenas flavirostris
Other Names: Paloma Morada Vientrioscura, Tzusuy

There are several species of pigeons in Belize; all are short legged, with a small head and bill, and a plump body. They are strong, fast fliers and hurtle past as if shot from cannons. A fairly shy bird, the Red-billed Pigeon lives mainly in the forests, although it is also found in the savannahs.

The bird is mainly dark, but its red bill is a good field mark if you can get close enough to see it or use binoculars. Red-billed pigeons feed on small fruits and berries, with mistletoe berries being a favorite. The female lays a single egg in a tree or shrub. Pigeons feed their young a special "pigeon's milk," which develops in the lining of both sexes' crops. Like mammal's milk, pigeon's milk is very high in fat, protein, and vitamins. Gradually the adults introduce other foods to the young, and production of the milk stops about the time the young leave the nest.

Ruddy Ground-Dove
Columbina talpacoti

Other Names: Tortolita Rojiza, Mukuy, Turtle Dove

Commonly found in cleared areas, the male Ruddy Ground-Dove is a cinnamon color while the female is brownish gray. These small doves are found in all parts of Belize except the cayes. They often become quite tame if not harassed and approach houses as they search the ground for seeds and insects. Ground doves are often called "turtle doves" in Belize.

Like many birds, the Ruddy Ground-Dove builds its nest during the dry season. The female sits on the nest to be and arranges bits of grass as the male brings them to her one by one. A shallow saucer-like form takes shape, and it becomes the home of two white eggs. The parents share incubation duties and both feed the young "pigeon's milk." The young can fly weakly at nine days, and leave the nest after about two weeks.

Blue Ground-Dove
Claravis pretiosa

Other Names: Tórtola Azul, Tuch Mukuy, Turtle Dove

In this ground-dove, the sexes are strongly dimorphic. Males are a lovely light blue, and females are a soft brown with darker wingbars. Often they can be seen flying close together and this combination—a blue bird and a brown bird—makes them easy to recognize. Ground doves are often called "turtle doves" in Belize.

The Blue Ground-Dove is found in fairly open areas along forest edges or secondary growth. It is often seen along roads. The Blue Ground-Dove's call is a single low "hoot!" which it may give every few seconds. It builds its nest only a few feet above the ground, well hidden among vines and dense growth. It is a delicate, almost frail structure made of vines, twiglets, and weed stems. Two pure white eggs are incubated for 14 days.

Olive-throated Parakeet

Aratinga nana

Other Names: Perico Pechisucio,
Xkili, Xk'ali'l, Aztec
Parakeet, Keetie

Sometimes called the "Aztec" parakeet, this small member of the parrot family is a familiar sight everywhere in Belize except the coasts and cayes. It is normally seen in flocks of at least two and up to 14 or more birds which shriek noisily as they fly. A Belizean name for it is "keetie."

"Parakeet" means small parrot and this bird shares all the characteristics of its larger family members. Parakeets are very social, preferring to remain with others of their kind. Their strong hooked beaks are well-adapted to cracking open tough seeds and nuts, and also useful as an extra "hand" in climbing. Mainly green in color, these birds are difficult to see when feeding in the tree tops on fruits and blossoms. Like all parrots, the Olive-throated Parakeet nests in tree cavities and lays white eggs. These birds are noisy, very social, and do not make good pets.

Scarlet Macaw
Ara macao

Other Names: Guacamaya
Roja, Moo, Ix Oop, Ah K'ota

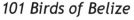

The Scarlet Macaw prefers higher elevations and tall forests along rivers and streams. Both the Guacamayo Bridge and the Macal River were named for this beautiful bird, but these days you would be lucky indeed to see even one. While the guacamayo can still be found in Belize, its numbers are not high. The Scarlet Macaw is a tragic victim of human greed over the years; too many have been taken for pets or hunted for sport or displaced due to habitat loss.

Macaws do not make good pets. They do not learn to speak well, and often become vicious; their strong bills a r e capable of doing serious damage. The best thing we could do for the few remaining Scarlet Macaws is to leave them alone and tell others not to molest them. Eventually they could recover from human persecution.

White-crowned Parrot

Pionus senilis

Other Names: Perico Cabeza Blanca, Xt'ut

This is the darkest and bluest of our parrots, and the only one with a white cap. The female is duller in color, and the blue stops on her upper breast. Like all parrots, it is very social and is almost always seen in large noisy flocks. It can be found in the forest canopy and sometimes in second growth.

Although in captivity it looks brilliant and colorful, the White-crowned Parrot is very well camouflaged while feeding in the treetops on fruits, seeds or nuts. Only its loud cries give it away. Like other parrots in Belize, it is a cavity nester. Highly social, it prefers the company of others of its kind. It is also very noisy, and not at all well suited to being a pet.

Yellow-headed Parrot

Amazona oratrix

Other Names: Loro Coroniamarillo, Yellow-head

Most people think the "Yellow-head" is the best talking parrot in Belize. These days they are seen more frequently as pets in cages—usually much too small for them—instead of flying free. Like all parrots in Belize, it is illegal to take them.

Unfortunately, there are fewer and fewer Yellow-heads because nesting trees are cut down to capture the young. As more trees are cut and removed, it becomes even more difficult for Yellow-heads to find a suitable tree to nest in. While flocks can be seen flying over Belize's savannahs, there are very few young birds with them. As the older birds eventually die, there are few younger birds to take their place as breeding adults. Although parrots are long lived, their kind will not survive if they cannot raise young.

The Yellow-head prefers to roost in pairs in tall pine trees in the pine ridge. During the early morning hours, it flies to the forests often along rivers where it feeds, returning to its roost at night. People should not take these birds nor cut down their nesting trees. Please give them a chance to successfully raise their young.

Squirrel Cuckoo
Piaya cayana
Other Names: Cuclillo Marrón, Kipcho, Pequam

Often seen on forest edges, the Squirrel Cuckoo gets its name from its ability to run and hop agilely along boughs and branches—rather like a squirrel. Called "pequam" in Belize, it is a slender and attractive bird with its rich cinnamon color and long graduated tail marked in black and white.

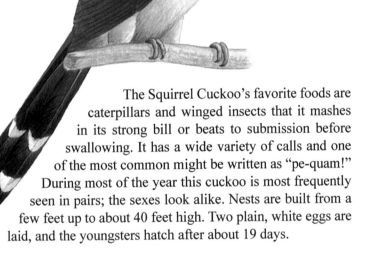

The Squirrel Cuckoo's favorite foods are caterpillars and winged insects that it mashes in its strong bill or beats to submission before swallowing. It has a wide variety of calls and one of the most common might be written as "pe-quam!" During most of the year this cuckoo is most frequently seen in pairs; the sexes look alike. Nests are built from a few feet up to about 40 feet high. Two plain, white eggs are laid, and the youngsters hatch after about 19 days.

Groove-billed Ani
Crotophaga sulcirostris

Other Names: Garrapatero Pijuy, Chick-bul, Cowboy

The "cowboy" gets its Belizean and Spanish names from its occasional habit of picking ticks from cattle. Groove-billed Anis are a familiar sight in pastures and cleared areas where they live in groups of two to fifteen or more.

Anis seem to enjoy each other's company as they perch on fences close together, grooming each other, and sunning themselves with never an argument. This close association extends to their communal nesting habits. A single large nest is built, and all the females lay their eggs in it. Both males and females take turns with incubation and feeding the nestlings. The devoted members of the group search the ground for insects and small lizards to feed the young.

Mottled Owl

Ciccaba virgata

Other Names: Búho Tropical (Americano), Icim

A forest dweller, this bird of prey hunts at night. Like all owls, the Mottled Owl has acute hearing and large, forward-facing eyes adapted to seeing in dim light. Soft feathers, another adaptation to night hunting, enable the owl to fly very quietly. The Mottled Owl does not have tufted feathers protruding from its head which give other species of owls the appearance of having "ears."

The Mottled Owl is probably the most common owl in Belize. Its wide variety of calls—some of them especially eerie and haunting—can be heard at twilight. Rodents and large insects are this bird's preferred foods. Mottled Owls nest in tree cavities and produce two dull white eggs.

Common Pauraque

Nyctidromus albicollis

Other Names: Tapacamino Pucuyo, Pujuy, Who-you

During the dry season, especially on moonlit nights, the "who-you" call of the Common Pauraque is a familiar sound. This nocturnal bird prefers open habitat next to farmlands, in savannahs and forest clearings, and along forest edges.

Caught in the headlights of an oncoming car, the eye shine of the Pauraque is ruby red. Otherwise, this bird is cloaked in dark colors except for the conspicuous white wing bars. Its usual method of hunting is to sit on the ground, propelling itself upward into the air to snatch an insect, then falling back to the same spot. The Pauraque has a tiny bill with rictal bristles on either side. Rictal bristles are specialized feathers that act as a sort of net to "herd" insects into its enormous mouth. The Pauraque builds no nest; instead it lays two eggs directly on the ground. Both parents care for the young.

Northern Potoo

Nyctibius jamaicensis

Other Names: Nictibio, Hap, Tree-nighthawk, Potoo

At first glance, this nightbird is often mistaken for an owl. With the same dark colors and soft feathers, it flies silently, blending into its habitat. It's most easily seen at night when its large yellow eyes glow red if caught in the light. Once called "tree-nighthawks," the creole name "potoo" eventually stuck.

The potoo sits on an upright perch or snag in open areas at night where it darts out after flying insects such as moths and beetles. It returns to its perch to devour them. During the day, the potoo prefers to perch in the shelter of the forest, and sometimes may even lie against its perch to avoid being seen.

Potoos are not great nest builders. Instead they find a depression in a tree or stump and in it lay a single egg without benefit of lining or other structure to protect it.

Vaux's Swift
Chaetura vauxi
Other Names: Vencejo Alirrápido, K'usam

Vaux's Swift can eat, sleep, and even gather nesting material as it flies through the air with the greatest of ease. Its weak and tiny feet are adapted only for clinging. Agile, fast, and high flying, "swift" is a fitting name for this most excellent aerialist. It is seen over forests, pastures, and even cities.

Built for speed, this bird has what is often referred to as a "cigar-shaped" body and spends much of its time in flight with other members of its species. It has a characteristic fluttering flight with rapid wing beats, and it seldom soars. Basically gray, it has a small bill opening into a wide mouth and catches insects on the wing. It builds a bracket-like nest in a hollow tree, gluing twigs together with sticky saliva; then lays four white eggs.

Long-billed Hermit
Phaethornis longirostris

Other Names: Ermitaño Común, Tsunuum

If a tiny helicopter buzzes up to you and gives a sharp squeak before zipping off, chances are it was a hummingbird. Common and extremely curious, the Long-tailed Hermit is found in lowland forests. The name "hermit" comes from the fact that it travels alone and is far ranging with no specific territory.

Hermits have long, curved bills especially adapted for feeding on heliconius flowers like the waha leaf or the wild ginger flower. With its long white-tipped tail, it is a graceful sight as it darts from flower to flower. Males form "leks" or courtship groups where they gather to attract a female. But the female alone builds the nest, made from plant fiber and anchored with spider webs, and she also raises the babies alone.

Rufous-tailed Hummingbird
Amazilia tzacatl

Other Names: Chupaflor Pechigris, Tsunuum

A common resident in gardens, the Rufous-tailed takes its name from its chestnut colored tail feathers. The male is glittering green and the female is identical but for her more gray-olive breast. This hummingbird especially likes red flowers like the hibiscus and will aggressively defend its flowers from other hummingbirds and even large insects like bees and butterflies. While often found in gardens, this hummingbird is truly widespread, occurring also in plantations, open scrub, and forest gaps.

Hummingbirds are not known for melodious song and Rufous-tails are no exception. An excited twitter or squeak is the most it can manage. Like other hummingbirds, the female undertakes nest building by herself, often in the thorn-protected citrus, where she raises two young.

Purple-crowned Fairy

Heliothryx barroti

Other Names: Chupaflor Enmascarado, Tsunuum

This hummer is especially beautiful with its blue-green back, snow white underparts, and purple crown. A light and graceful flier, it is a resident of the canopy in primary forests and will sometimes swoop down to take a closer look at you before darting off.

Purple-crowned Fairies have a short, sharp bill adapted for piercing the base of flowers to get at the nectar. Often they can be seen high overhead buzzing from flower to flower when the Mayflower is in bloom. Another good way to get a look at them is when they come down to bathe in a mud puddle or along a shallow stream. They build tiny cone-shaped nests at a height of at least 30 feet, often at the end of a slender branch as protection from predators.

Violaceous Trogon
Trogon violaceus

Other Names: Trogón Pechiamarillo Colibarrado, Ramatutu

Trogons are beautiful birds found only in the tropics. Visitors to Belize are usually excited to see them. Belize has four trogon species: two with yellow bellies, like the Violaceous, and two with red bellies. Violaceous refers to the purplish gloss on the upper breast of the male, who also has a yellow eye ring. The female resembles him but is paler without the eye ring.

Trogons are often found sitting very quietly and despite their bright colors, they may be hard to see amidst the forest greenery. The Violaceous Trogon prefers forest edges, plantations, or lowland tropical forest. Like all trogons, it is primarily a frugivore, or fruit eater. It also takes some protein in the form of insects and has even been seen perching near a wasp nest taking wasps on the wing. This species digs a nest cavity in a termite mound using its bill and feet. The termites seal up the nest hole after the trogons' youngsters have left.

Slaty-tailed Trogon

Trogon massena

Other Names: Trógon Colioscuro

Of Belize's two red-bellied trogon species, the Slaty-tailed is the larger at about 12 inches. The male has an orange eye ring and bill and a plain "slaty tail." The female resembles him, but is duller in color. This species prefers wet primary forest and is rarely seen in second-growth forest. Slaty-tailed Trogons are normally found alone unless it is the breeding season when they are in pairs.

Like other trogons, the Slaty-tailed's diet is fruit and insects which they can take on the wing. As frugivores, these trogons play an important role in the forest. When the fruits are digested, the hard seeds pass through their bodies and are distributed, helping to reseed the forest.

"Trogon" comes from a Greek word meaning "the gnawer," which no doubt refers to the bird's method of excavating a nest cavity in soft decaying wood or termite nests. Three to four bluish to whitish eggs are laid, and both parents feed and care for the young.

Blue-crowned Motmot

Momotus momota

Other Names: Momoto Mayor, Toh, Jut Jut, Bukpic, Good Cook

Motmots are a family of beautiful birds found only in the tropics. The Blue-crowned is large, with a strong bill, and it sits quietly in trees, often switching its long tail back and forth like a pendulum. The tail is especially distinctive because the bird strips bare a small area near the end, leaving rounded racquets at the tips. Male and female look alike. A soft "hoot hoot" call gives it the Mayan name "jut jut" and its Belizean name "good cook."

Main foods for the Motmot are fruits, large insects, and small reptiles. It lives in lowland forests as well as drier forests and even gardens. Motmots nest in burrows, often in a natural cavity found in banks or at Maya sites. These burrows are deepened and enlarged by both sexes and can extend as far as five to 14 feet. The females usually produce three glossy white eggs.

79

Keel-billed Motmot

Electron carinatum

Other Names: Momoto Piquiancho

The Keel-billed Motmot is a much less common member of the Motmot family. It is thought to be nearly extinct in Guatemala and Mexico, and only small populations survive in Belize, apparently exclusively in the higher elevations of the Maya Mountains. This is a lovely bird which Belizeans can be very proud still makes its home here.

The Keel-billed is distinguished from the Blue-crowned Motmot by its smaller size and heavier bill with chestnut at its base. It lacks the Blue-crown's red eye. The Keel-billed's call is very different from that of other motmots sounding like a hoarse "qwaa qwaa." This is often the first call in the dawn chorus, sounding out even before the sun is up. Like other motmots, it perches quietly watching for food, then darts with lightning speed to snatch a cicada or katydid or other large insect which it beats several times against its perch before swallowing.

Ringed Kingfisher

Ceryle torquata

Other Names: Martín Pescador Grande

There are two large species of kingfishers in Belize. The Belted is a North American migrant, spending a good part of the year in Belize's mild climate. The Ringed Kingfisher is a year-round resident here and a much larger bird. These two species share similar coloration. Both sexes of the Ringed have rust-colored bellies, but, for a switch, the female has the gaudier plumage with a gray chest band as well.

Frequently seen along rivers, streams, and lagoons, kingfishers often sit motionlessly in plain sight. They are usually alone or in pairs. When a kingfisher spots a potential meal of a fish or a small frog, it often hovers above it, then darts into the water for the capture. Kingfishers have no song as such—only a harsh rattling chatter. Related to motmots, kingfishers also excavate burrows in banks and usually produce four to six white eggs.

81

Green Kingfisher

Chloroceryle americana

Other Names: Martín Pescador Menor

This small kingfisher occurs from southern Texas to central Argentina, and prefers small shady streams with heavy, low hanging vegetation. The Green Kingfisher can often be seen flying over the water giving its "tick tick" call and flashing its white outer tail feathers. The male has a rusty breast band, while the female has a green spotted band.

Like other kingfishers, it excavates a burrow for nesting. In fact, the two forward-facing toes are partially fused, an adaptation which aids in scooping dirt from the burrow. Juvenile kingfishers first practice dives on floating sticks and leaves, before graduating to small fish and other aquatic creatures just below the water's surface. Prey is taken to a perch, sometimes beaten, then swallowed head first.

Rufous-tailed Jacamar

Galbula ruficauda

Other Names: Gálbula Común

Looking like a giant hummingbird, the Rufous-tailed Jacamar can be found perching quietly in dense forests with tangled vegetation. Brilliantly colored in glittering green, the female differs from the male only in that her throat is buff rather than pure white. Jacamars are relatives of the Kingfishers.

Jacamars dart from their perches after butterflies, dragonflies, and other large insects, in often spectacular aerial acrobatics. It is thought that the length of the bill prevents the bird from being stung by enabling it to hold stinging insects at a safe distance from its face. The captured insect is taken back to the perch and its wings are beaten off before it is devoured. Both sexes share the chores of digging a burrow, often in a steep bank, and caring for the youngsters.

Keel-billed Toucan

Ramphastos sulfuratus

Other Names: Tucán Piquiverde, Bill Bird

Familiar to most of us as the National Bird of Belize, the Keel-billed Toucan is the largest of the three toucan species occurring here. Its beautiful rainbow-colored bill gives it the nickname "bill bird." Although you may wonder how the toucan can fly with such a heavy-looking bill, the bill is actually very light. This large bird has a heavy flapping flight and utters a "creek creek" sound, like that of a frog.

Toucans are found throughout Belize's hardwood forests and prefer the canopy where they often feed in small flocks. As frugivores, they are important in seed dispersal throughout the forest. Not entirely vegetarian, they also take other birds' eggs and nestlings and the occasional lizard. Toucans nest in tree holes, both high and low, and lay one to four dull white eggs.

Acorn Woodpecker
Melanerpes formicivorus

Other Names: Carpintero Careto

This woodpecker is very distinctive with bold black-and-white markings and clown-like face. The males have an all red crown while the females have black on the crown and then red.

Its name tells us its most important food, the acorn, so these woodpeckers are always found in areas with oak trees. In Belize, this would be on the savannahs and especially in the Mountain Pine Ridge where oaks are abundant. This species also lives in southwestern North America where it stores acorns for the cold winter months when insects, another favored food, are not as available. Although insects are almost always available in Belize, this woodpecker still stores acorns in crevices, wedged between bark, and in specially drilled holes in dead trees.

This is a very social bird, often seen in family groups consisting of a pair with their offspring from the last two or three years. The entire family helps with raising the young and requires tall dead trees for their nest holes.

Golden-fronted Woodpecker
Melanerpes aurifrons

Other Names: Colonte, Carpenter

Here in Belize the Golden-fronted Woodpecker has no golden on it; in fact, the males show quite a bit of red. This is because it is a subspecies in which there is some variation. Here, the golden color is not present as in other populations. Like other woodpeckers, the Golden-fronted has an "undulating" flight, meaning it seems to rise and fall in waves when it flies.

The "carpenter" appears in open wooded areas, and scattered trees near homes and is often a familiar sight. As with all woodpeckers, it has a stiff tail which acts as a prop while climbing trees which it clasps with strong toes. It hammers its bill into the tree and uses it as a chisel, then extracts insects with its long tongue. It also eats sap and occasionally fruit. Not surprisingly, tree holes are used as nests where normally four white eggs are laid.

Pale-billed Woodpecker

Campephilus guatemalensis

Other Names: Carpintero Grande Cabecirrojo, Colonté, Father Red Cap

The largest woodpecker in Belize is the handsome Pale-billed. Its Belizean name, "father red cap," refers to its striking red head and black and white plumage. It is found in the hardwood forests where it requires mature trees to make its living. Like other woodpeckers, it probes and scales bark from tree trunks in search of insects. This benefits the tree by helping to regulate insects which may be harmful to it. The Pale-billed is also known to take fruit.

Females differ from males only in that they have black foreheads rather than all red bushy crests. Besides tapping trees in search of insects, the rhythmic "knock knock" also defines territories and warns other Pale-bills of boundary lines. Pale-billed Woodpeckers nest in tree holes and lay two glossy, pure white eggs.

Plain Xenops

Xenops minutus

Other Names: Picolezna Bigotiblanco, Jana'-sinik

Another resident of Belize's hardwood forests is a small brown bird known as the Plain Xenops. No more than five inches in size and distinguished by its white "moustache" markings, this bird is not shy and can often be seen hanging upside down on branches searching for insects, an activity for which its upside-down bill is well- suited.

The Xenops belongs to a family known as ovenbirds, most of which are brown or gray. None of the ovenbirds is especially noted for song, and the Plain Xenops is no exception. It makes a chipping or hissing sound. While many ovenbirds build clay, oven-like nests, the Xenops nests in a tree hole making a cup nest lined with plant fibers during the dry season. Two white eggs are laid.

Wedge-billed Woodcreeper
Glyphorynchus spirurus

Other Names: Trepador Piquicorto

The Wedge-billed Woodcreeper is the smallest of the nine species of woodcreepers in Belize. It is sometimes confused with the Plain Xenops because of its similar size and habitat preference, but its spotted breast makes it quite different as does its behavior. The Wedge-billed Woodcreeper is very common in the forests around the Maya site, Caracol. Woodcreepers have strong feet which allow them to clutch tree bark as they hitch themselves upwards. A strong spiny tail acts as a prop to support the bird as it scans the bark for insects and spiders.

This little woodcreeper nests at various heights, ranging from 20 feet down to buttressed roots and occasionally ground level. It uses a natural cavity which it lines with fibrous materials. Both adults care for the youngsters by bringing them small insects and keeping the nest clean by removing droppings.

Ivory-billed Woodcreeper
Xiphorhynchus flavigaster
Other Names: Trepador Dorsirrayado Mayor, Takaj-ché

The Ivory-billed is a larger member of the woodcreeper family. Its name comes from its long, light-colored bill which is very slightly curved. It is one of the most common woodcreepers found in Belize's hardwood forests. Like all woodcreepers in this neotropical group, it is warm brown in color and has an undulating flight like that of a woodpecker.

The Ivory-bill searches along branches and tree trunks looking for food. Slowly and carefully it moves along, searching with its eyes rather than probing with its bill as a woodpecker might. After it has moved up the tree and searched to its satisfaction, it flies to the next tree where it begins the process again. Large insects such as beetles and crickets make up the bulk of its diet. It has a distinctive melodious whistle and is thought to nest in tree holes or cavities.

Barred Antshrike

Thamnophilus doliatus

Other Names: Batará Barrado, Balan-ch'ich'

Commonly found in dry forests, savannahs, and thickety places, the Barred Antshrike has a distinctive call: long, drawn out and ending in a hiccup. It's more often heard than seen which is unfortunate because it is a very attractive bird. The male is striped black and white, while the female is rusty brown.

With its heavy hooked beak, the antshrike searches dense thickets for insects which make up its diet. The Barred Antshrike is a member of a family called antbirds which are found only in the forests of Central and South America. Antbirds get their name because they follow army ant swarms—not to eat the ants, but to catch the insects which the ant columns flush out. Both members of the Antshrike pair build a nest which is suspended from a forked branch and care for the young together.

Black-faced Antthrush
Formicarius analis

Other Names: Mexican Antthrush, Hormiguero Carinegro, Xbech'lu'um

Another ant follower, this bird has a stout body, strong legs, and a short tail. Its whistled call is distinctive and it often responds if you whistle back. Typical of many of the antbirds, it has bare blue skin around the eyes. This is thought to suggest the giant eye spots of a mammal and thus frighten would-be predators.

While it might sun itself in a patch of light, this antthrush is a true forest dweller and is never caught in the open. Favored foods are spiders, insects, small lizards, and frogs which the bird searches for in the leaf litter on the forest floor. Sometimes antbirds follow mammals like peccary or warrie who stir up the leaf litter on the forest floor and so help the bird to find insects. The Black-faced Antthrush is a cavity nester, selecting a site in a hollow trunk or root. It is thought that it remains with the same mate for life.

Royal Flycatcher

Onychorhynchus coronatus

Other Names: Mosquero Real

At first glance, this resident of Belize's dense hardwood forests appears rather dull. That is because its magnificent crest is nearly invisible when folded flat as it is most of the time. When giving its display, the bird spreads its crest into a colorful fan while swaying its head side to side. The male's crest is a spectacular scarlet, with a black border and purple spots. The female's is similar except that it is golden.

An insect eater, this flycatcher has a broad flat bill adapted for snatching insects on the wing. Royal Flycatcher nests look like a windblown tangle of vines, twigs, and leaves. They

can be as long as two to six feet and hang from a slender twig, often over running water. This arrangement offers the bird good protection from predators while raising its young.

Vermilion Flycatcher
Pyrocephalus rubinus

Other Names: Cardenalito

The male of this small species fully deserves his name. No other flycatcher in Belize is such a bright red. The male has a bushy crest and black upper parts contrasting with his red head, throat, and belly. The female is much more subdued with brownish upper parts and pinkish belly. Young males resemble females but their bellies are much redder.

You can most often see this flycatcher on slender branches, or perched on fences in open areas, particularly in savannah areas. From these perches it darts out to snap up insects. This little bird ranges from the southwestern United States all the way to Argentina, and is a year-round resident in Belize.

Vermilion Flycatcher males have a showy courtship display. The bright red male bird flutters up as high as 50 feet with his crest and breast feathers puffed out, all the while calling. He hovers midair and moves forward in what has been called a "butterfly flight." All this effort is undertaken to impress a watching female.

Great Kiskadee

Pitangus sulphuratus

Other Names: Luis Bienteveo, Xtakay

Almost all of us know the Great Kiskadee, a resident of open country. It does well in cleared areas near homes and is often found along pools or streams. Named for its call "kis-ka-dee!" it is similar in color pattern to the Social Flycatcher although it is larger and usually alone. It also resembles the Boat-billed Flycatcher which has a broader, heavier bill and is smaller in size. Its Maya name refers to yellow-bellied flycatchers in general and thus is applied to several different species.

The Kiskadee's slightly curved hooked bill is designed for catching insects on the wing, but it also takes fruits. Kiskadees can sometimes be seen searching along streams for small fish which they try to catch by shallow dives into the water. The Kiskadee's nest is bulky and dome-shaped, made from long grasses, weeds, and roots with its doorway mostly hidden from view. It lays three or four white eggs lightly spotted with brown.

Tropical Kingbird
Tyrannus melancholicus

Other Names: Tirano Tropical Común, Xtakay

Very common and easily seen in open areas and in the savannahs, this is another member of the flycatcher family. Although not brightly colored, the Tropical Kingbird has a hidden orange crown patch which it flashes in displays to other kingbirds. The Kingbird is usually seen on an open perch where it watches the area and then darts out after insects. The rictal bristles at the sides of its large broad bill are typical of flycatchers; they act as a "net" which helps in the capture of insects.

Kingbirds can be bold and aggressive toward hawks and jays which are considered potential nest predators. Although much smaller, the kingbird will drive them away fearlessly. A nest is constructed of dried grasses formed into a bulky bowl. It holds two or three pale buff eggs with brownish blotches.

Masked Tityra

Tityra semifasciata

Common names: Titira Piquinegro, Ppilankeuel

If you hear a pig-like grunting coming from the treetops it is probably a Masked Tityra, whose strange call doesn't sound a bit like a bird. This species is very arboreal, remaining in the crowns of tall trees which sometimes overlook open areas. It is easily seen, often in areas near villages.

The male is gray and white with a bare red area around the eye; the female is more brownish, and is easily recognized. This bird is related to both the flycatchers and another family of birds called the cotingas and shares features of each group.

Tityras live in pairs and are cavity nesters, often arguing noisily with woodpeckers for the same holes anywhere from about 10 to 40 feet up. The nest is a cup, lined with leaves and bark and small twigs. The female produces two brownish-cream eggs with dark brown marbling and black spots.

Red-capped Manakin
Pipra mentalis

Other Names: Pipra Cabecirroja

There are about 50 members in the manakin family, which is found only in Central and South America. Most manakin species feature brilliantly colored males, and dull green females. We have three species in Belize. The Red-capped male is surely one of our most attractive forest birds with its flame-red head. The bird is found only in Belize's hardwood forests, where it eats fruits and insects.

Most manakins have an elaborate courtship display to attract a female. In the case of the Red-capped, the males "dance," flying from perch to perch, squeaking and making s n a p p i n g noises with their wings—sounding rather like a dry stick being broken. All this is done in hopes of attracting a female. Males practice endlessly in their courtship groups, stepping up their dancing when a female is watching. But it is the female alone that builds a shallow cup nest and lines it with plant fibers. She usually lays two eggs and raises the young alone.

Yucatan Vireo
Vireo magister

Other Names: Vireo Yucateco

The word "vireo" comes from the Latin word meaning "to be green," and most members of the vireo family have at least some green on them. Vireos are also characterized by a hook at the tip of the beak. The Yucatan Vireo, as its name suggests, is found only in the Yucatán Peninsula which includes the coasts and islands of Belize ranging down to about Honduras. This species is fairly common in mangrove areas but is also found in gardens and thickets. It is about six inches in size, with a dark eye stripe and yellowish underparts.

Vireos forage in trees and shrubs snatching insects from leaves and also taking berries. The nest is carefully woven of grasses and fibers and suspended from a forked branch. The female incubates the eggs for a little less than two weeks. Both parents care for the young, continuing 20-30 days after the young have left the nest.

Brown Jay

Cyanocorax morio

Other Names: Urarca Pea, Paap, Piam Piam

With its noisy "piam! piam!" warning call, the Brown Jay often gives the first alert of intruders. Brown Jays travel in flocks of six to 10 birds and are very adaptable as they can be found in all sorts of habitats: cleared areas, second growth, hardwood forests. Like most other jays, they eat just about anything, including fruit, insects, and even other birds' nestlings or eggs. That is why you can often see smaller birds vigorously driving a Brown Jay away.

Brown Jays build their nests of sticks in a platform lined with smaller sticks and finally fibers. Studies have shown that normally the oldest pair in the flock lays eggs, with other females occasionally adding their eggs to the communal nest. All flock members take turns incubating the eggs and feeding the young. When they are just out of the nest, the young have a yellow eye-ring, legs, and feet which darken in time.

Gray-breasted Martin

Progne chalybea

Other Names: Golondrina Grande
Pechipálida, Ah Cuzam

A familiar "town" bird, the Gray-breasted Martin has long, narrow wings, a short, compact body, and quick and graceful flight. Short-legged with small weak feet, the Martin's short, flat bill opens wide to scoop up flying insects while on the wing. Its sleek design makes it well adapted to its life in wide-open skies.

While many martins migrate to the Pacific coast of Mexico, some are year round residents and nest in Belize. Often martins nest colonially using tree cavities or rocky cliffs. Perhaps you may have noticed that they also nest in nooks and crannies on the outside of people's houses. The female builds the nest while the male supplies her with material. Three or four eggs are laid and the young must be fully mature before they can leave the nest and take to life on the wing.

Band-backed Wren

Campylorhynchus zonatus

Other Names: Carrasquita

A large and noisy member of the wren family, this bird is often seen near our homes where cover such as trees and shrubs is available. The species seems to prefer palms and tall trees but is also found in forests and along rivers.

Male and female look alike, both attractively striped. Most wrens are musical, but not this one; it only chatters noisily with other members of its family group. This is a highly social bird and is seldom seen alone. Families often stay together and continue to use the large globular nest as a dormitory long after the nestlings are fledged. The bird's diet consists of insects and spiders.

Spot-breasted Wren

Thryothorus maculipectus

Other Names: Troglodita Pechimanchada, Xan-cotí, Katy-yu-baby-di-cry

Wrens are short-winged, active birds, and most are known for their beautiful songs. A Belizean name is "Katy-yu-baby-di-cry." The Spot-breasted Wren keeps to tangled thickets in forested areas and is quite common in Belize.

This wren's beautiful song is sung antiphonally, or in a "duet." Male and female each sing its own part so well that it sounds as if only one bird were singing. The wren's slender bill is slightly curved to probe crevices and turn leaves for the insects which make up the bird's diet. Male and female form a monogamous pair and together build a snug nest of grass stems and weeds with a side entrance. They line it with soft fibers and feathers to shelter three or four white eggs with brown splotching. Nests are often located in the crotch of a tree or shrub up to 20 feet above the ground. After the young are grown, the nests are often still used as sleeping quarters.

Long-billed Gnatwren
Ramphocaenus melanurus

Other name: Sílvido Picudo

R elated to the thrushes and gnatcatchers, the Long-billed Gnatwren is found in dense thickets and undergrowth along cleared forest edges. More often heard than seen, its song is a series of trilled whistles, often very loud.

This small active bird flits and hops about in viney tangles in search of small insects and spiders which are captured using its extremely long, slender bill. The Gnatwren remains in pairs throughout the year and constructs a thick-walled open cup nest using small twigs and dried

leaves. The nest is lined with fibers and grasses held together with cobwebs and is sometimes only six inches off the ground. Two white eggs sprinkled with cinnamon are laid. The young hatch naked and helpless but leave the nest in twelve to fifteen days.

Wood Thrush

Hylocichla mustelina

Other name: Zorzalito Maculado

A part-time resident of Belize, the Wood Thrush lives in the forest understory in humid areas. Like many thrushes, it has large, dark eyes, and hops along the forest floor where it searches the leaf litter for insects, spiders, and earthworms. Occasionally it eats berries.

This bird migrates to Canada and the eastern and central parts of the United States where it builds its nest and raises its young during the few warm months. Then it makes the long trip back to Belize and other parts of Central America usually returning year after year to the same territory. A few years ago, a Wood Thrush netted and banded in Belize's Chiquibul National Park was recaptured in Maine near the United States' border with Canada. When forests are cut, Wood Thrushes must find new territories or they become very vulnerable to predators.

Clay-colored Thrush

Turdus grayi

Other Names: Zorzal Pardo, Xk'ok, Cusco

Closely related to the Wood Thrush, this bird is a year-round resident of Belize, found in cultivated areas such as gardens, pastures, and plantations. It also inhabits second growth. Clay-colored Thrushes eat fruit, and like Wood Thrushes, also search the ground for earthworms and other insects.

Thrushes are lovely songsters. The Clay-colored Thrush with its clear, whistled song is especially noticeable during the breeding season. The bird is medium-sized, and males and females look alike. The nest may be found in the crotch of a tree or on top of a post. Sturdy and well made, it is an open bowl with an inner wall of mud mixed with plant fibers. The outer wall is made of plant materials and the inside cup is lined. The female lays two or three eggs speckled with reddish brown. A Belizean name is "cusco."

Gray Catbird
Dumetella carolinensis

Other Names: Mímido Gris

Appropriately named for its cat-like "meow!" this bird has a variety of songs since it is closely related to the mockingbirds. Its courtship song isn't heard in Belize though because it is a migrant species. Each year it flies to southern Canada and the eastern and central United States to build its nest and raise a family during the warm summer months there.

The catbird is rather secretive and usually shows itself only at dawn and dusk, otherwise spending its time in thick undergrowth. It adapts to a wide variety of habitats in Belize, including cleared areas, forests, and even some of the cayes which offer the thicket it prefers. The catbird's diet consists of insects as well as fruits and berries.

Black Catbird

Melanoptila glabrirostris

Other Names: Mímido Negro, Siwa-ban

The Black Catbird is a secretive creature that prefers the thickets alongside coastlines and on some of the cayes. Its range once extended along the Yucatán Peninsula from Quintana Roo, Mexico, to Honduras, but unfortunately its preferred habitat is disappearing because of rapid development.

Black Catbirds are sometimes confused with the common and noisy Great-tailed Grackle, which can be seen just about everywhere on Ambergris and Cay Caulker. But the Black Catbird is smaller--a very pretty, glossy, blue-black bird with a red eye and shy habits. Its musical song is heard most frequently beginning in February at the start of its breeding season. Because the Black Catbird cannot adjust to "town life," natural vegetation must be preserved if the species is to survive. Three reserves on Caye Caulker—two private and one public—protect habitat for the siwa-ban and other species of the threatened littoral forest of the cayes.

Magnolia Warbler
Dendroica magnolia

Other Names: Chipe Colifaja

L eaving the coniferous north woods of Canada and the northeastern United States, this little warbler arrives in Belize with males, females, and young of the year looking much alike. By springtime though, the males have molted just in time to head north for the breeding season with striking black, gray, and yellow plumage.

Here in Belize, this little bird can be seen in thickets, open groves, and woodlands, often alone but sometimes with mixed flocks of other small birds. Its normal method of feeding is to snatch insects and spiders from the upper surfaces of leaves, fanning its tail, which has a distinctive broad white band. Before departing Belize, it eats tremendous amounts of insects to build up stores of fat and the energy necessary to carry it thousands of miles to its breeding grounds.

American Redstart
Setophaga ruticilla

Other name: Pavito Migratorio, Candelita, Little Torch

Candelita or "little torch" well describes the lively movements of this little warbler as it pirouettes from branch to branch fanning its tail. Nearly everyone has seen the small but strikingly colored black-and-orange males at Christmas time. Females and immature birds are much less colorful, feathered in gray and yellow.

The first wave of migrating male redstarts reaches Florida by early April. The birds continue to push northward until they reach their breeding grounds in the eastern U.S. and southern Canada, where they compete for territories in readiness for the females soon to join them. When nesting is completed, they begin their return to Belize and other parts of Central America as early as mid-July. Look for this species in forested areas and tall shrubs in all parts of Belize.

Red-throated Ant-Tanager
Habia fuscicauda

Other name: Tangara Rojisucia

Common and numerous, this noisy bird is found in flocks of four to eight birds. The male is a dull red with a red throat patch and a concealed red crown patch, while the female is a golden brown and her throat and crown patches are deep yellow. Young birds resemble females.

Ant-tanagers are found in the understories of primary forests as well as second growth and along rivers and streams. They provide a good early-warning system, scolding loudly at any disturbance, often from a hidden position with an occasional dash to an open perch. Ant-tanagers eat fruits and sometimes follow swarms of army ants, eating insects which the ants stir out of the leaf litter.

The nest is a loosely woven cup nest of fine fibers usually not more than 12 feet up in the forest undergrowth or sometimes in dense second growth. Three unmarked eggs are normally laid.

111

Red-legged Honeycreeper

Cyanerpes cyaneus

Other name: Mielero Dorsioscuro

During much of the year, the male honeycreeper is especially lovely in purplish blue, with a turquoise crown and brilliant lemon yellow under the wings. But during the nonbreeding season, he dons "eclipse" plumage which resembles the dull green of the female. Its bright red legs and curved bill, adapted to nectar feeding, combine to give this bird its name.

Honeycreepers forage in the crowns of tall trees in small flocks often mixed with other species. Occasionally they come into second-growth areas and to lower levels where they can be more easily seen. They prefer berries and small fruits, nectar and insects. They are frequently seen in pairs and are not noted for their song. A small thin cup nest is made of fine fibers, rootlets, and grasses amid the foliage of slender branches. Two white eggs speckled with pale brown are laid.

White-collared Seedeater

Sporophila torqueola

Other name: Semillerito Collarejo, Ricey

This tiny finch is common in weedy, open areas, abandoned fields, and in grasses along marshes and near gardens. The male is at his most attractive during the breeding season with his bright black, buff, and white markings and musical, canary-like song. The female by contrast is a plain brown with two wingbars.

Like most finches, this bird has a stubby cone-shaped bill. Traveling in small flocks, these seedeaters are a common sight wherever land has been cleared and allowed to go into weeds. Association with rice fields gives it the Belizean name, "ricey." Occasionally seedeaters take small fruits and insects. Their nest is a delicately woven cup of grasses and rootlets bound with spider web and found two to ten feet high in trees. Two or three blue-gray eggs mottled with brown and black are normally laid.

113

Black-headed Saltator

Saltator atriceps

Other Names: Saltator Cabecinegro, Tsapin

This common bird is quite large, nearly ten inches, and is familiar to many people around their gardens. It also inhabits dense forests, thickets, and tangles. While not brightly colored, it is attractively marked with yellow-green upper parts with light gray underneath. The sexes look alike. This is one of three species of saltators found in Belize and is distinguished from the others by its larger size and black head. Saltators are members of the Emberizid family—sparrows and finches—and have the heavy, cone-shaped bill characteristic of this group.

Saltators travel in small family-sized flocks, which are often noisy and conspicuous. But even with its bold call, it is still a relatively shy bird. Preferred foods include seeds, small fruits, insects, and sometimes flower buds. It builds a bulky nest at low levels and produces two bluish eggs with black markings at the larger end.

Indigo Bunting
Passerina cyanea

Other name: Colorín Azul

Many of us here in Belize may wonder why this little finch carries the name "indigo," a deep shade of blue. After all, during most of its stay here in Belize, it has light brown upper parts and is buffy underneath. But in late April, as the time draws near for these buntings to migrate north, the males begin to regain their deep blue breeding plumage.

Indigo Buntings prefer scrub areas with high weeds, and weedy fields. They forage in flocks of about 20 eating mainly seeds for which their cone-shaped finch bill is well designed. Nesting takes place from southeastern Canada through the southeastern part of the United States. Indigo buntings often raise more than one brood per season.

Melodious Blackbird

Dives dives

Other Names: Tordo Cantor, Pich

There are several all-black birds found in Belize, and this one is familiar in plantations, cultivated areas, second growth, and along wooded edges. It is smaller with a shorter tail than the Great-tailed Grackle which is often found in the same sorts of areas. Males are a sleek, glossy black, about ten inches in size, while females are somewhat smaller and duller black. Both have brown eyes, another way to distinguish this species from the grackle male which has a bright yellow eye.

Sometimes a pest, the Melodious Blackbird likes corn and grains, as well as insects which it hunts while bobbing its head and striding on the ground. Its name implies its wide range of song, which includes piercing whistles. Nests are usually located six to twenty feet high, often in citrus trees where thorns protect the nesting birds and young. The nest is a deeply woven cup lined with fine grasses and rootlets. This blackbird's three eggs of light blue are marked with large and small black spots.

Yellow-tailed Oriole

Icterus mesomelas

Other Names: Chorcha de Cola Amarilla, Yuyum

There are several colorful species of orioles in Belize, and all of them are quite attractive with yellow and black, or orange and black markings. The fairly common Yellow-tailed can be easily distinguished because it is the only oriole with a yellow-sided tail. Male and female look the same.

This species is found in second-growth areas and around villages where the male's pretty song is familiar. Sometimes his mate will answer him in short phrases. Yellow-tailed Orioles like dense thickets and roadsides, and often forage in pairs for insects, spiders, and sometimes fruit. Orioles are well known for their finely woven basket-like nests; however, the Yellow-tailed's nest is more cup-like. Normally three eggs are laid.

117

Montezuma Oropendola
Psarocolius montezuma

Other name: Zacua Mayor, Xhom Bzan, Yellowtail

Known in Belize as "yellowtail," its common name means golden ("oro") tail ("pendola") also. This large relative of the orioles is found in forests and open woodland. The males reach nearly 20 inches in length while the females are about 16 inches. Both are chestnut colored with black and have colorful bills and facial markings.

Once heard, the gurgling call is unforgettable. The bird gives it an all out effort, falling forward and upside down on his perch to utter it. Other calls sound like a rusty hinge or broken engine squeaking.

Favored foods are a variety of fruits, nectar and insects. Oropendolas are colonial nesters, often selecting a giant ceiba tree from which they suspend tightly woven pouches two to six feet long. There is an opening in the top and two eggs are laid on a lined surface.

Yellow-throated Euphonia

Euphonia hirundinacea

Other Names: Calandrita de Garganta Amarilla, Chinchin-
bakal

S mall and colorful, this pretty little tanager likes more open areas
along forest edges as well as second growth and gardens. The male
is especially attractive; his bright yellow throat, breast and belly contrast
sharply with shiny, blue-black feathers. The female is a rather dull green.
A similar species, the Scrub Euphonia, is also found in Belize. Male
Scrub Euphonias are distinguished by a black bib rather than a yellow
throat.

Euphonias normally travel in pairs or small family groups. They
search mid and upper levels of trees for insects and fruits. Male and
female work together to build an untidy looking roofed nest from all
sorts of fine vegetation and dried grasses, but it falls to the female alone
to incubate the eggs.

119

Glossary

Adaptation—The way a bird had adjusted historically to a feature in its life. Protective coloration, a specially curved bill for feeding, large eyes for improved night vision, are some examples of adaptations.

Arboreal—Living in trees.

Carrion—The flesh of a dead animal, favored food of vultures.

Colonial—Birds which roost or nest in a group with members of their own species, and sometimes other species. It is thought this gives them a measure of protection against predators.

Clutch—Referring to the group of eggs an individual bird lays and broods.

Crop—An enlargement of the gullet used for food storage in some families of birds.

Dimorphism—Refers to birds that have two distinct forms; often the male bird looks very different from the female bird.

Endangered—Any species which is in danger of extinction throughout all or a significant part of their range." From the Endangered Species Act of 1973.

Evolve—The process by which a species has changed over time in response to environmental pressures.

Extinct—Species which no longer exist whether due to natural or human causes.

Family—A major category which groups similar types of birds.

Field Mark—A characteristic by which a bird may be distinguished "in the field" from another bird that may look very similar.

Fledgling—A young bird with feathers, having outgrown its baby down, but still dependent on its parents.

Forage—To search for food.

Frugivore—A fruit eater.

Genera *incertae sedis*—Classification of the following birds is uncertain.

Genus—A category grouping similar species of birds within a given family. The plural is "genera."

Habitat—A part of the environment having the features necessary for a bird to survive, such as adequate cover, food, and water.

Incubate—To sit upon eggs to keep them at the proper temperature so that they develop and hatch.

Invertebrates—Animals without back bones. This category includes insects, spiders and many aquatic creatures.

Lek—A place where male birds gather to perform display rituals to attract females.

Migrant—A bird that moves seasonally from one place to another.

Monogamous—Remaining paired and faithful to one mate.

Morph—A form, variation, or phase which might occur within a certain species.

New World—The landmasses of the Western Hemisphere.

Neotropics—A geographic region that begins in Mexico and includes South America.

Nocturnal–Refers to creatures that are active at night.

Olivaceous—A greenish brown color used to describe the plumage of some birds.

Ornithologist—A scientist whose area of study is birds.

Pantropical—Occurring throughout the tropics.

Polyandrous—Refers to species in which the female bird mates with several males who in turn incubate the eggs. Polyandry occurs in only a few species.

Plumage—The feathers that cover a bird's body.

Predation—The killing and eating of one animal by another.

Range—The geographical area where a species occurs.

Raptor—A bird of prey that uses their talons and beak for holding and tearing the flesh of an animal it has killed. Hawks, eagles and owls are raptors.

Regurgitate—To bring up partially digested food from the stomach.

Rictal—Stiff hair-like feathers that extend over the bird's mouth, and act as a "net" in capturing insects.

Roost—A place where birds collect to rest or sleep by day or night. A roost can be on the ground or in the treetops.

Secondary Growth—Plants that colonize land after it has been cleared, like the Cecropia, or trumpet tree.

Species—A unique type of animal or plant.

Talons—The long sharp claws of a bird of prey.

Territory—An area defended from other members of their species where a bird may feed, raise their young, etc.

Thermals—Columns of warm air rising from the earth's heated surface.

Vertebrates —Animals with back bones.

Bibliography

American Ornithologists' Union. 1998. *The A.O.U. Check-list of North American Birds*. 7ᵗʰ Edition. Lawrence, KA: Allen Press, Inc.

American Ornithologists' Union. 2007. Forty-eighth supplement to the American Ornithologists' Union Check-list of North American Birds. *Auk* 124:1109–1115.

American Ornithologists' Union. 2008. Forty-ninth supplement to the American Ornithologists' Union Check-list of North American Birds. *Auk* 125:758–768.

Barlow, S. C.; Caddick, G. B. 1989. *Report on the Status of the Scarlet Macaw, Ara macao, in Belize, Central America.* Report for the Center for the Study of Tropical Birds

Belize Audubon Society. *Half Moon Caye Natural Monument*. Information brochure.

Blake, E. R. *Birds of Mexico*. 1953. Chicago, IL: University of Chicago Press

Bijleveld, C. and M. McField. 2000. *Report on 10 years of activities in Belize (Central America)*.1–12.

Campbell, B; Lack, E., Editors. 1985. *A Dictionary of Birds*. Vermillion, SD: Buteo Books

Davis, L. I. 1972. Birds *of Mexico and Central America.* Austin, TX: University of Texas Press

de Schauensee, R. M., Phelps, W. H., Jr. 1978. *A Guide to the Birds of Venezuela*. Princeton, NJ: Princeton University Press

Dunning, J. S. 1982. *South American Land Birds*. Newtown Square, PA: Harrowood Books

Edwards, E. P. 1989. *A Field Guide to the Birds of Mexico*. Second Edition. Sweet Briar, VA

Farrand, J., Jr., Editor. 1983. *The Audubon Society Master Guide to Birding*. Vols. I, II, III. New York, NY: Alfred A. Knopf

Goodwin, D. *Pigeons and Doves of the World*. 1970. Ithaca, NY: Comstock Publishing Associates

Griscom, L., Ed. *The Warblers of America*. 1979. Garden City, NY: Doubleday and Company, Inc.

Hardy, J. W.; Coffey, B. B.; Reynard, G. C. 1989. *Voices of the New World Nightjars and their Allies*. Gainesville, FL: Ara Records

Harrison, C. J. O., Editor. 1978. *Bird Families of the World*. New York, NY: Harry Abrams, Inc.

Hartshorn, G. et al. 1984. *Belize Country Environmental Profile*. USAID

Howell, S.N.G., 1994. The specific status of the black-faced antthrushes in Middle America. *Cotinga*:20–25.

Howell, S.N.G. and S. Webb. 1995. *A Guide to the Birds of Mexico and Northern Central America*. Oxford University Press. Oxford.

Isler, M. L.; Isler, P. R. 1987. The *Tanagers Natural History, Distribution, and Identification*. Washington D.C.: Smithsonian Institution Press

Janzen, D. H., editor. 1983. *Costa Rican Natural History*. Chicago, IL: University of Chicago Press

Jones, H. L. 2003. *Birds of Belize*. 1st ed. Austin, TX: University of Texas Press

Lancaster, D. A. 1970. Breeding behavior of the Cattle Egret in Columbia. *Living Bird*, 9:167–194.

Land, H. C. 1970. *Birds of Guatemala*. Wynnewood, PA: Livingston Publishing Co.

Leahy, C. 1982. *The Birdwatcher's Companion*. New York, NY: Hill and Wang

Martin, G. 1990. *Birds by Night*. London: Poyser

MacKinnon de Montes, B. 1989. *100 Common Birds of the Yucatán Peninsula*. Cancun, Quintana Roo, Mexico: Amigos de Sian Ka'an.

Miller, B. W., Tilson, R. L. 1985. Snail Kite Kleptoparasitism of Limpkins. *Auk* 102(1):170–171;

Miller, B. W., Miller, C. M. 1992. Distributional Notes and New Species Records for Birds in Belize. *Occasional Papers of The Belize Natural History Society*, 1(1):6–25

Miller, C. M.; Miller, B. W. 1991. *Exploring the Rainforest at Chan Chich Lodge, Belize*. Gallon Jug, Belize: Chan Chich Lodge.

Miller, Bruce W. and Miller, Carolyn M. Ornithology in Belize Since 1960. *Wilson Bulletin*. 1998; 110(4)544–558.

Miller, B. W. and Miller, C. M. 2007. The Belize Important Bird Areas Project. Gallon Jug, Belize. 48–27 pp.

Peterson, R. T.; Chalif, E. L. 1973. *A Field Guide to Mexican Birds*. Boston, MA: Houghton Mifflin Company

Rappole, J. H. et. al. 1989. Wintering Wood Thrush movements and mortality in southern Veracruz. *Auk* 106:402–410

Ridgeley, R. S.; Gwynne, J. A. 1989. *A Guide to the Birds of Panama*. Princeton, NJ: Princeton University Press

Robbins, C. S.; Bruun, B.; Zim, H. S. 1966. *Birds of North America*. New York, NY: Golden Press

Russell, S. M. 1964. A Distributional Study of the Birds of British Honduras. *Ornith. Monogr.* 1. Amer. Ornith. Union

Sada, A. M. et. al. Agosto 1987. *Nombres en Castellano para las Aves Mexicanas*. Xalapa,Ver.: Instituto Nacional de Investigaciones Sobre Recursos Bióticos

Scott, S. L., editor. 1983. *Birds of North America*. Washington, D.C.: National Geographic Society.

Siwa-ban Nature Preserve. Caye Caulker, Belize. Information brochure.

Skutch, A. F. 1972. Studies of Tropical American Birds. Cambridge, MA: Nuttall *Ornithological Club*, No. 10.

Skutch, A. F. 1981. New Studies of Tropical American Birds. Cambridge, MA:Nuttall *Ornithological Club,* No. 19

Skutch, A. F. 1983. *Birds of Tropical America*. Austin, TX: University of Texas Press.

Smithe, F. B.; Trimm, H. W. 1966. *Birds of Tikal*. Garden City, NY: Natural History Press.

Stiles, G. F., Skutch, A. F. 1989. *Birds of Costa Rica*. Ithaca, NY: Comstock Publishing Associates

Weich, F. 1980. *Birds of Prey of the World*. Hamburg and Berlin, Germany: Verlag Paul Parey

Wood, D. S. et al. 1986. *Checklist of the Birds of Belize*. Special publication No. 12. Pittsburg, PA: Carnegie Museum of Natural History

Young, W. Ford. 1981. Some Local Names of Belizean Birds. *Belize Audubon Society Bulletin*, Vol. 13, No. 3

Appendix I: Checklist—Birds of Belize

The common names and arrangement of this list follows American Ornithologists Union (1998) and all subsequent updates through the 49th supplement (2008). The species have been updated from Jones (2003) as well as a few others since then. A few species are shown as "*incertae sedis.*" This means they are placed "approximately" in the list for the time being, at the end of the family to which they seem to be most closely related. With more study, ornithologists will be able to make a determination in the future.

Tinamous—*Tinamidae*

Great Tinamou	*Tinamus major*
Little Tinamou	*Crypturellus soui*
Thicket Tinamou	*Crypturellus cinnamomeus*
Slaty-breasted Tinamou	*Crypturellus boucardi*

Swans, Geese and Ducks—*Anatidae*

Black-bellied Whistling Duck	*Dendrocygna autumnalis*
Fulvous Whistling Duck	*Dendrocygna bicolor*
Greater White-fronted Goose	*Anser albifrons*
Snow Goose	*Chen caerulescens*
Muscovy Duck	*Cairina moschata*
American Wigeon	*Anas americana*
Mallard	*Anas platyrhynchos*
Blue-winged Teal	*Anas discors*
Cinnamon Teal	*Anas cyanoptera*
Northern Shoveler	*Anas clypeata*
Northern Pintail	*Anas acuta*
Green-winged Teal	*Anas crecca*
Ring-necked Duck	*Aythya collaris*
Lesser Scaup	*Aythya affinis*
Hooded Merganser	*Lophodytes cucullatus*
Red-breasted Merganser	*Mergus serrator*
Masked Duck	*Nomonyx dominicus*

Curassows and Guans—*Cracidae*

Plain Chachalaca	*Ortalis vetula*
Crested Guan	*Penelope purpurascens*
Great Curassow	*Crax rubra*

Turkeys—*Phasianidae*

Ocellated Turkey	*Meleagris ocellata*

Quails – *Odontophoridae*
    Black-throated Bobwhite   *Colinus nigrogularis*
    Spotted Wood-Quail   *Odontophorus guttatus*
    Singing Quail   *Dactylortyx thoracicus*
Grebes—*Podicipedidae*
    Least Grebe   *Tachybaptus dominicus*
    Pied-billed Grebe   *Podilymbus podiceps*
Flamingos—*Phoenicopteridae*
    Greater Flamingo   *Phoenicopterus ruber*
Shearwaters & Petrels—*Procellariidae*
    Sooty Shearwater   *Puffinus griseus*
    Manx Shearwater   *Puffinus puffinus*
    Audubon's Shearwater   *Puffinus iherminieri*
Tropicbirds—*Phaethonidae*
    White-tailed Tropicbird   *Phaethon lepturus*
Boobies and Gannets—*Sulidae*
    Masked Booby   *Sula dactylatra*
    Brown Booby   *Sula leucogaster*
    Red-footed Booby   *Sula sula*
Pelicans—*Pelecanidae*
    American White Pelican   *Pelecanus erythrorhynchos*
    Brown Pelican   *Pelecanus occidentalis*
Cormorants – *Phalacrocoracidae*
    Neotropic Cormorant   *Phalacrocorax brasilianus*
    Double-crested Cormorant   *Phalacrocorax auritus*
Anhingas—*Anhingidae*
    Anhinga   *Anhinga anhinga*
Frigatebirds—*Fregatidae*
    Magnificent Frigatebird   *Fregata magnificens*
Bitterns and Herons—*Ardeidae*
    Pinnated Bittern   *Botaurus pinnatus*
    American Bittern   *Botaurus lentiginosus*
    Least Bittern   *Ixobrychus exilis*
    Bare-throated Tiger-Heron   *Tigrisoma mexicanum*
    Great Blue Heron   *Ardea herodias*
    Great Egret   *Ardea alba*
    Snowy Egret   *Egretta thula*
    Little Blue Heron   *Egretta caerulea*
    Tricolored Heron   *Egretta tricolor*
    Reddish Egret   *Egretta rufescens*

Cattle Egret	*Bubulcus ibis*
Green Heron	*Butorides virescens*
Agami Heron	*Agamia agami*
Black-crowned Night-Heron	*Nycticorax nycticorax*
Yellow-crowned Night-Heron	*Nyctanassa violaceus*
Boat-billed Heron	*Cochlearius cochlearius*

Ibises and Spoonbills—*Threskiornithidae*

White Ibis	*Eudocimus albus*
Scarlet Ibis	*Eudocimus ruber*
Glossy Ibis	*Plegadis falcinellus*
Roseate Spoonbill	*Ajaia ajaja*

Storks—*Ciconiidae*

Jabiru	*Jabiru mycteria*
Wood Stork	*Mycteria americana*

American Vultures—*Cathartidae*

Black Vulture	*Coragyps atratus*
Turkey Vulture	*Cathartes aura*
Lesser Yellow-headed Vulture	*Cathartes burrovianus*
King Vulture	*Sarcoramphus papa*

Kites, Eagles, Hawks and Allies—*Accipitridae*

Osprey	*Pandion haliaetus*
Gray-headed Kite	*Leptodon cayanensis*
Hook-billed Kite	*Chondrohierax uncinatus*
Swallow-tailed Kite	*Elanoides forficatus*
White-tailed Kite	*Elanus leucurus*
Snail Kite	*Rostrhamus sociabilis*
Double-toothed Kite	*Harpagus bidentatus*
Mississippi Kite	*Ictinia mississippensis*
Plumbeous Kite	*Ictinia plumbea*
Black-collared Hawk	*Busarellus nigricollis*
Northern Harrier	*Circus cyaneus*
Sharp-shinned Hawk	*Accipiter striatus*
Cooper's Hawk	*Accipiter cooperii*
Bicolored Hawk	*Accipiter bicolor*
Crane Hawk	*Geranospiza caerulescens*
White Hawk	*Leucopternis albicollis*
Common Black-Hawk	*Buteogallus anthracinus*
Great Black-Hawk	*Buteogallus urubitinga*
Solitary Eagle	*Harpyhaliaetus solitarius*

Roadside Hawk	*Buteo magnirostris*
Broad-winged Hawk	*Buteo platypterus*
Gray Hawk	*Buteo nitida*
Short-tailed Hawk	*Buteo brachyurus*
Swainson's Hawk	*Buteo swainsoni*
White-tailed Hawk	*Buteo albicaudatus*
Zone-tailed Hawk	*Buteo albonotatus*
Red-tailed hawk	*Buteo jamaicensis*
Crested Eagle	*Morphnus guianensis*
Harpy Eagle	*Harpia harpyja*
Black Hawk-Eagle	*Spizaetus tyrannus*
Ornate Hawk-Eagle	*Spizaetus ornatus*
Black-and-white Hawk-Eagle	*Spizaetus melanoleucus*

Falcons – *Falconidae*

Barred Forest-Falcon	*Micrastur ruficollis*
Collared Forest-Falcon	*Micrastur semitorquatus*
Crested Caracara	*Caracara cheriway*
Laughing Falcon	*Herpetotheres cachinnans*
American Kestrel	*Falco sparverius*
Merlin	*Falco columbarius*
Aplomado Falcon	*Falco femoralis*
Bat Falcon	*Falco rufigularis*
Orange-breasted Falcon	*Falco deiroleucus*
Peregrine Falcon	*Falco peregrinus*

Rails, Gallinules and Coots—*Rallidae*

Ruddy Crake	*Laterallus ruber*
Gray-breasted Crake	*Laterallus exilis*
Black Rail	*Laterallus jamaicensis*
Clapper Rail	*Rallus longirostris*
Rufous-necked Wood-Rail	*Aramides axillaris*
Gray-necked Wood-Rail	*Aramides cajanea*
Uniform Crake	*Amaurolimnas concolor*
Sora	*Porzana carolina*
Yellow-breasted Crake	*Porzana flaviventer*
Spotted Rail	*Pardirallus maculatus*
Purple Gallinule	*Porphyrio martinica*
Common Moorhen	*Gallinula chloropus*
American Coot	*Fulica americana*

Sungrebes—*Heliornithidae*
    Sungrebe   *Heliornis fulica*
Limpkins—*Aramidae*
    Limpkin   *Aramus guarauna*
Plovers – *Charadriidae*
    Southern Lapwing   *Vanellus chilensis*
    Black-bellied Plover   *Pluvialis squatarola*
    American Golden Plover   *Pluvialis dominica*
    Collared Plover   *Charadrius collaris*
    Snowy Plover   *Charadrius alexandrinus*
    Wilson's Plover   *Charadrius wilsonia*
    Semipalmated Plover   *Charadrius semipalmatus*
    Piping Plover   *Charadrius melodus*
    Killdeer   *Charadrius vociferus*
Oystercathers—*Haematopodidae*
    American Oystercatcher   *Haematopus palliatus*
Stilts and Avocets—*Recurvirostridae*
    Black-necked Stilt   *Himantopus mexicanus*
    American Avocet   *Recurvirostra americana*
Jacanas—*Jacanidae*
    Northern Jacana   *Jacana spinosa*
Sandpipers and Allies—*Scolopacidae*
    Spotted Sandpiper   *Actitis macularia*
    Solitary Sandpiper   *Tringa solitaria*
    Greater Yellowlegs   *Tringa melanoleuca*
    Willet   *Tringa semipalmatus*
    Lesser Yellowlegs   *Tringa flavipes*
    Upland Sandpiper   *Bartramia longicauda*
    Whimbrel   *Numenius phaeopus*
    Long-billed Curlew   *Numenius americanus*
    Hudsonian Godwit   *Limosa haemastica*
    Marbled Godwit   *Limosa fedoa*
    Ruddy Turnstone   *Arenaria interpres*
    Red Knot   *Calidris canutus*
    Sanderling   *Calidris alba*
    Semipalmated Sandpiper   *Calidris pusilla*
    Western Sandpiper   *Calidris mauri*
    Least Sandpiper   *Calidris minutilla*

White-rumped Sandpiper	*Calidris fuscicollis*
Baird's Sandpiper	*Calidris bairdii*
Pectoral Sandpiper	*Calidris melanotos*
Dunlin	*Calidris alpina*
Stilt Sandpiper	*Calidris himantopus*
Buff-breasted Sandpiper	*Tryngites subruficollis*
Short-billed Dowitcher	*Limnodromus griseus*
Long-billed Dowitcher	*Limnodromus scolopaceus*
Wilson's Snipe	*Gallinago delicate*
Wilson's Phalarope	*Phalaropus tricolor*
Red-necked Phalarope	*Phalaropus lobatus*

Gulls, Terns and Skimmers—*Laridae*

Black-legged Kitiwake	*Rissa tridactyla*
Bonaparte's Gull	*Chroicocephalus philadelphia*
Laughing Gull	*Leucophaeus atricilla*
Franklin's Gull	*Leucophaeus pipixcan*
Black-tailed Gull	*Larus crassirostris*
Ring-billed Gull	*Larus delawarensis*
Herring Gull	*Larus argentatus*
Great Black-backed Gull	*Larus marinus*
Brown Noddy	*Anous stolidus*
Black Noddy	*Anous minutus*
Sooty Tern	*Onychotrion fuscatus*
Bridled Tern	*Onychotrion anaethetus*
Least Tern	*Sternula antillarum*
Gull-billed Tern	*Gelochelidon nilotica*
Caspian Tern	*Hydroprogne caspia*
Black Tern	*Chlidonias niger*
Roseate Tern	*Sterna dougallii*
Common Tern	*Sterna hirundo*
Forster's Tern	*Sterna forsteri*
Royal Tern	*Thalasseus maxima*
Sandwich Tern	*Thalasseus sandvicensis*
Black Skimmer	*Rynchops niger*

Skuas & Jaegers—*Stercorariidae*

Great Skua	*Stercorarius skua*
Pomarine Jaeger	*Stercorarius pomarinus*
Parasitic Jaeger	*Stercorarius parasiticus*

131

Pigeons and Doves—*Columbidae*

Rock Pigeon	*Columba livia*
Pale-vented Pigeon	*Patagioenas cayennensis*
Scaled Pigeon	*Patagioenas speciosa*
White-crowned Pigeon	*Patagioenas leucocephala*
Red-billed Pigeon	*Patagioenas flavirostris*
Short-billed Pigeon	*Patagioenas nigrirostris*
Eurasian Collared-Dove	*Streptopilia decaocto*
White-winged Dove	*Zenaida asiatica*
Zenaida Dove	*Zenaida aurita*
Mourning Dove	*Zenaida macroura*
Inca Dove	*Columbina inca*
Common Ground-Dove	*Columbina passerina*
Plain-breasted Ground-Dove	*Columbina minuta*
Ruddy Ground-Dove	*Columbina talpacoti*
Blue Ground-Dove	*Claravis pretiosa*
White-tipped Dove	*Leptotila verreauxi*
Gray-headed Dove	*Leptotila plumbiceps*
Caribbean Dove	*Leptotila jamaicensis*
Gray-chested Dove	*Leptotila cassini*
Ruddy Quail-Dove	*Geotrygon montana*

Parrots—*Psittacidae*

Olive-throated Parakeet	*Aratinga nana*
Scarlet Macaw	*Ara macao*
Brown-hooded Parrot	*Pyrilia haematotis*
White-crowned Parrot	*Pionus senilis*
White-fronted Parrot	*Amazona albifrons*
Yellow-lored Parrot	*Amazona xantholora*
Red-lored Parrot	*Amazona autumnalis*
Mealy Parrot	*Amazona farinosa*
Yellow-headed Parrot	*Amazona oratrix*
Yellow-naped Parrot	*Amazona auropalliata*

Cuckoos and Allies—*Cuculidae*

Squirrel Cuckoo	*Piaya cayana*
Yellow-billed Cuckoo	*Coccyzus americanus*
Mangrove Cuckoo	*Coccyzus minor*
Black-billed Cuckoo	*Coccyzus erythropthalmus*
Striped Cuckoo	*Tapera naevia*
Pheasant Cuckoo	*Dromococcyx phasianellus*

Smooth-billed Ani	*Crotophaga ani*
Groove-billed Ani	*Crotophaga sulcirostris*

Barn-Owls—*Tytonidae*

Barn Owl	*Tyto alba*

Typical Owls—*Strigidae*

Vermiculated Screech-Owl	*Megascops guatemalae*
Crested Owl	*Lophostrix cristata*
Spectacled Owl	*Pulsatrix perspicillata*
Great Horned Owl	*Bubo virginianus*
Central American Pygmy-Owl	*Glaucidium griseiceps*
Ferruginous Pygmy-Owl	*Glaucidium brasilianum*
Burrowing Owl	*Athene cunicularia*
Mottled Owl	*Ciccaba virgata*
Black-and-white Owl	*Ciccaba nigrolineata*
Stygian Owl	*Asio stygius*
Short-eared Owl	*Asio flammeus*
Striped Owl	*Pseudoscops clamator*

Goatsuckers—*Caprimulgidae*

Short-tailed Nighthawk	*Lurocalis semitorquatus*
Lesser Nighthawk	*Chordeiles acutipennis*
Common Nighthawk	*Chordeiles minor*
Common Pauraque	*Nyctidromus albicollis*
Yucatan Poorwill	*Nyctiphrynus yucatanicus*
Chuck-will's Widow	*Caprimulgus carolinensis*
Tawny-collared Nightjar	*Caprimulgus salvini*
Yucatan Nightjar	*Caprimulgus badius*
Whip-poor-will	*Caprimulgus vociferus*

Potoos—*Nyctibiidae*

Northern Potoo	*Nyctibius jamaicensis*

Swifts—*Apodidae*

White-chinned Swift	*Cypseloides cryptus*
Chestnut-collared Swift	*Streptoprocne rutila*
White-collared Swift	*Streptoprocne zonaris*
White-naped Swift	*Streptoprocne semicollaris*
Chimney Swift	*Chaetura pelagica*
Vaux's Swift	*Chaetura vauxi*
White-throated Swift	*Aeronautes saxatalis*
Lesser Swallow-tailed Swift	*Panyptila cayennensis*

Hummingbirds—*Trochilidae*

Band-tailed Barbthroat	*Threnetes ruckeri*
Long-billed Hermit	*Phaethornis longirostris*
Stripe-throated Hermit	*Phaethornis striigularis*
Scaly-breasted Hummingbird	*Phaeochroa cuvierii*
Wedge-tailed Sabrewing	*Campylopterus curvipennis*
Violet Sabrewing	*Campylopterus hemileucurus*
White-necked Jacobin	*Florisuga mellivora*
Brown Violetear	*Colibri delphinae*
Green-breasted Mango	*Anthracothorax prevostii*
Black-crested Coquette	*Lophornis helenae*
Canivet's Emerald	*Chlorostilbon canivetii*
Violet-crowned Woodnymph	*Thalurania colombica*
Blue-throated Goldentail	*Hylocharis eliciae*
White-bellied Emerald	*Amazilia candida*
Azure-crowned Hummingbird	*Amazilia cyanocephala*
Rufous-tailed Hummingbird	*Amazilia tzacatl*
Buff-bellied Hummingbird	*Amazilia yucatanensis*
Cinnamon Hummingbird	*Amazilia rutila*
Striped-tailed Hummingbird	*Eupherusa eximia*
Magnificent Hummingbird	*Eugenes fulgens*
Purple-crowned Fairy	*Heliothryx barroti*
Long-billed Starthroat	*Heliomaster longirostris*
Ruby-throated Hummingbird	*Archilochus colubris*
Rufous Hummingbird	*Selasphorus rufus*

Trogons—*Trogonidae*

Black-headed Trogon	*Trogon melanocephalus*
Violaceous Trogon	*Trogon violaceus*
Collared Trogon	*Trogon collaris*
Slaty-tailed Trogon	*Trogon massena*

Motmots—*Momotidae*

Tody Motmot	*Hylomanes momotula*
Blue-crowned Motmot	*Momotus momota*
Keel-billed Motmot	*Electron carinatum*

Kingfishers—*Alcedinidae*

Ringed Kingfisher	*Ceryle torquata*
Belted Kingfisher	*Ceryle alcyon*
Amazon Kingfisher	*Chloroceryle amazona*
Green Kingfisher	*Chloroceryle americana*
American Pygmy Kingfisher	*Chloroceryle aenea*

Puffbirds—*Bucconidae*
    White-necked Puffbird   *Notharchus macrorhynchos*
    White-whiskered Puffbird   *Malacoptila panamensis*
Jacamars—*Galbulidae*
    Rufous-tailed Jacamar   *Galbula ruficauda*
Toucans—*Ramphastidae*
    Emerald Toucanet   *Aulacorhynchus prasinus*
    Collared Aracari   *Pteroglossus torquatus*
    Keel-billed Toucan   *Ramphastos sulfuratus*
Woodpeckers—*Picidae*
    Acorn Woodpecker   *Melanerpes formicivorus*
    Black-cheeked Woodpecker   *Melanerpes pucherani*
    Yucatan Woodpecker   *Melanerpes pygmaeus*
    Golden-fronted Woodpecker   *Melanerpes aurifrons*
    Yellow-bellied Sapsucker   *Sphyrapicus varius*
    Ladder-backed Woodpecker   *Picoides scalaris*
    Smoky-brown Woodpecker   *Veniliornis fumigatus*
    Golden-olive Woodpecker   *Piculus rubiginosus*
    Chestnut-colored Woodpecker   *Celeus castaneus*
    Lineated Woodpecker   *Dryocopus lineatus*
    Pale-billed Woodpecker   *Campephilus guatemalensis*
Ovenbirds—*Furnariidae*
    Tawny-throated Leaftosser   *Sclerurus mexicanus*
    Scaly-throated Leaftosser   *Sclerurus guatemalensis*
    Rufous-breasted Spinetail   *Synallaxis erythrothorax*
    Scaly-throated Foliage-gleaner   *Anabacerthia variegaticeps*
    Buff-throated Foliage-gleaner   *Automolus ochrolaemus*
    Plain Xenops   *Xenops minutus*
Woodcreepers—*Dendrocolaptidae*
    Tawny-winged Woodcreeper   *Dendrocincla anabatina*
    Ruddy Woodcreeper   *Dendrocincla homochroa*
    Olivaceous Woodcreeper   *Sittasomus griseicapillus*
    Wedge-billed Woodcreeper   *Glyphorhynchus spirurus*
    Strong-billed Woodcreeper   *Xiphocolaptes*
                                    promeropirhynchus
    Northern Barred Woodcreeper   *Dendrocolaptes sanctithomae*
    Ivory-billed Woodcreeper   *Xiphorhynchus flavigaster*
    Spotted Woodcreeper   *Xiphorhynchus erythropygius*
    Streak-headed Woodcreeper   *Lepidocolaptes souleyetii*

Antbirds—*Thamnophilidae*

Great Antshrike	*Taraba major*
Barred Antshrike	*Thamnophilus doliatus*
Western Slaty-Antshrike	*Thamnophilus atrinucha*
Russet Antshrike	*Thamnistes anabatinus*
Plain Antvireo	*Dysithamnus mentalis*
Slaty Antwren	*Myrmotherula schisticolor*
Dot-winged Antwren	*Microrhopias quixensis*
Dusky Antbird	*Cercomacra tyrannina*
Bare-crowned Antbird	*Gymnocichla nudiceps*

Antbirds—*Formicariidae*

Black-faced Antthrush	*Formicarius analis*

Tyrant Flycatchers—*Tyrannidae*

Tyrannulets and Elaenias—*Elaeniinae*

Yellow-bellied Tyrannulet	*Ornithion semiflavum*
Northern Beardless-Tyrannulet	*Camptostoma imberbe*
Greenish Elaenia	*Myiopagis viridicata*
Caribbean Elaenia	*Elaenia martinica*
Yellow-bellied Elaenia	*Elaenia flavogaster*
Ochre-bellied Flycatcher	*Mionectes oleagineus*
Sepia-capped Flycatcher	*Leptopogon amaurocephalus*
Paltry Tyrannulet	*Zimmerius vilissimus*

Tody-Tyrants and Flatbills—*Platyrinchinae*

Northern Bentbill	*Oncostoma cinereigulare*
Slate-headed Tody-Flycatcher	*Poecilotriccus sylvia*
Common Tody-Flycatcher	*Todirostrum cinereum*
Eye-ringed Flatbill	*Rhynchocyclus brevirostris*
Yellow-olive Flycatcher	*Tolmomyias sulphurescens*
Stub-tailed Spadebill	*Platyrinchus cancrominus*

Pewees and Allies—*Fluvicolinae*

Royal Flycatcher	*Onychorhynchus coronatus*
Ruddy-tailed Flycatcher	*Terenotriccus erythrurus*
Sulphur-rumped Flycatcher	*Myiobius sulphureipygius*
Olive-sided Flycatcher	*Contopus cooperi*
Greater Pewee	*Contopus pertinax*
Western Wood-Pewee	*Contopus sordidulus*
Eastern Wood-Pewee	*Contopus virens*
Tropical Pewee	*Contopus cinereus*
Yellow-bellied Flycatcher	*Empidonax flaviventris*
Acadian Flycatcher	*Empidonax virescens*

136

Alder Flycatcher	*Empidonax alnorum*
Willow Flycatcher	*Empidonax traillii*
White-throated Flycatcher	*Empidonax albigularis*
Least Flycatcher	*Empidonax minimus*
Black Phoebe	*Sayornis nigricans*
Eastern Phoebe	*Sayornis phoebe*
Vermilion Flycatcher	*Pyrocephalus rubinus*

Kingbirds and Allies—*Tyranninae*

Bright-rumped Attila	*Attila spadiceus*
Rufous Mourner	*Rhytipterna holerythra*
Yucatan Flycatcher	*Myiarchus yucatanensis*
Dusky-capped Flycatcher	*Myiarchus tuberculifer*
Great Crested Flycatcher	*Myiarchus crinitus*
Brown-crested Flycatcher	*Myiarchus tyrannulus*
Great Kiskadee	*Pitangus sulphuratus*
Boat-billed Flycatcher	*Megarynchus pitangua*
Social Flycatcher	*Myiozetetes similis*
Streaked Flycatcher	*Myiodynastes maculatus*
Sulphur-bellied Flycatcher	*Myiodynastes luteiventris*
Piratic Flycatcher	*Legatus leucophaius*
Tropical Kingbird	*Tyrannus melancholicus*
Couch's Kingbird	*Tyrannus couchii*
Cassin's Kingbird	*Tyrannus vociferans*
Eastern Kingbird	*Tyrannus tyrannus*
Gray Kingbird	*Tyrannus dominicensis*
Scissor-tailed Flycatcher	*Tyrannus forficatus*
Fork-tailed Flycatcher	*Tyrannus savana*

Genera *incertae sedis*

Thrush-like Schiffornis	*Schiffornis turdina*
Rufous Piha	*Lipaugus unirufus*
Speckled Mourner	*Laniocera rufescens*
Cinnamon Becard	*Pachyramphus cinnamomeus*
White-winged Becard	*Pachyramphus polychopterus*
Gray-collared Becard	*Pachyramphus major*
Rose-throated Becard	*Pachyramphus aglaiae*
Masked Tityra	*Tityra semifasciata*
Black-crowned Tityra	*Tityra inquisitor*

Cotingas—*Cotingidae*

| Lovely Cotinga | *Cotinga amabilis* |

Manakins—*Pipridae*
    White-collared Manakin   *Manacus candei*
    Red-capped Manakin   *Pipra mentalis*
Vireos—*Vireonidae*
    White-eyed Vireo   *Vireo griseus*
    Mangrove Vireo   *Vireo pallens*
    Yellow-throated Vireo   *Vireo flavifrons*
    Plumbeous Vireo   *Vireo plumbeus*
    Blue-headed Vireo   *Vireo solitarius*
    Hutton's Vireo   *Vireo huttoni*
    Warbling Vireo   *Vireo gilvus*
    Philadelphia Vireo   *Vireo philadelphicus*
    Red-eyed Vireo   *Vireo olivaceus*
    Yellow-green Vireo   *Vireo flavoviridis*
    Black-whiskered Vireo   *Vireo altiloquus*
    Yucatan Vireo   *Vireo magister*
    Tawny-crowned Greenlet   *Hylophilus ochraceiceps*
    Lesser Greenlet   *Hylophilus decurtatus*
    Green Shrike-Vireo   *Vireolanius pulchellus*
    Rufous-browed Peppershrike   *Cyclarhis gujanensis*
Jays—*Corvidae*
    Green Jay   *Cyanocorax yncas*
    Brown Jay   *Cyanocorax morio*
    Yucatan Jay   *Cyanocorax yucatanicus*
Swallows—*Hirundinidae*
    Purple Martin   *Progne subis*
    Gray-breasted Martin   *Progne chalybea*
    Tree Swallow   *Tachycineta bicolor*
    Mangrove Swallow   *Tachycineta albilinea*
    Northern Rough-winged Swallow   *Stelgidopteryx serripennis*
    Bank Swallow   *Riparia riparia*
    Cliff Swallow   *Petrochelidon pyrrhonota*
    Cave Swallow   *Hirundo fulva*
    Barn Swallow   *Hirundo rustica*
Wrens—*Troglodytidae*
    Band-backed Wren   *Campylorhynchus zonatus*
    Spot-breasted Wren   *Thryothorus maculipectus*
    Carolina Wren   *Thryothorus ludovicianus*
    Plain Wren   *Thryothorus modestus*

House Wren	*Troglodytes aedon*
Sedge Wren	*Cistothorus platensis*
Marsh Wren	*Cistothorus palustris*
White-bellied Wren	*Uropsila leucogastra*
White-breasted Wood-Wren	*Henicorhina leucosticta*
Nightingale Wren	*Microcerculus philomela*

Gnatcatchers—*Sylviidae*
Long-billed Gnatwren	*Ramphocaenus melanurus*
Blue-gray Gnatcatcher	*Polioptila caerulea*
Tropical Gnatcatcher	*Polioptila plumbea*

Solitaires, Thrushes, and Allies—*Turdidae*
Eastern Bluebird	*Sialia sialis*
Brown-backed Solitaire	*Myadestes occidentalis*
Slate-colored Solitaire	*Myadestes unicolor*
Veery	*Catharus fuscescens*
Gray-cheeked Thrush	*Catharus minimus*
Swainson's Thrush	*Catharus ustulatus*
Wood Thrush	*Hylocichla mustelina*
Clay-colored Thrush	*Turdus grayi*
White-throated Thrush	*Turdus assimilis*
American Robin	*Turdus migratorius*

Mockingbirds and Catbirds—*Mimidae*
Gray Catbird	*Dumetella carolinensis*
Black Catbird	*Melanoptila glabrirostris*
Tropical Mockingbird	*Mimus gilvus*

Pipits—*Motacillidae*
American Pipit	*Anthus rubesdens*

Waxwings—*Bombycillidae*
Cedar Waxwing	*Bombycilla cedrorum*

Wood Warblers—*Parulidae*
Blue-winged Warbler	*Vermivora pinus*
Golden-winged Warbler	*Vermivora chrysoptera*
Tennessee Warbler	*Vermivora peregrina*
Orange-crowned Warbler	*Vermivora celata*
Nashville Warbler	*Vermivora ruficapilla*
Virginia's Warbler	*Vermivora virginiae*
Northern Parula	*Parula americana*
Tropical Parula	*Parula pitiayumi*
Yellow Warbler	*Dendroica petechia*

Chestnut-sided Warbler	*Dendroica pensylvanica*
Magnolia Warbler	*Dendroica magnolia*
Cape May Warbler	*Dendroica tigrina*
Black-throated Blue Warbler	*Dendroica caerulescens*
Yellow-rumped Warbler	*Dendroica coronata*
Black-throated Gray Warbler	*Dendroica nigrescens*
Golden-cheeked Warbler	*Dendroica chrysoparia*
Black-throated Green Warbler	*Dendroica virens*
Townsend's Warbler	*Dendroica townsendi*
Hermit Warbler	*Dendroica occidentalis*
Blackburnian Warbler	*Dendroica fusca*
Yellow-throated Warbler	*Dendroica dominica*
Grace's Warbler	*Dendroica graciae*
Pine Warbler	*Dendroica pinus*
Prairie Warbler	*Dendroica discolor*
Palm Warbler	*Dendroica palmarum*
Bay-breasted Warbler	*Dendroica castanea*
Blackpoll Warbler	*Dendroica striata*
Cerulean Warbler	*Dendroica cerulea*
Black-and-white Warbler	*Mniotilta varia*
American Redstart	*Setophaga ruticilla*
Prothonotary Warbler	*Protonotaria citrea*
Worm-eating Warbler	*Helmitheros vermivorus*
Swainson's Warbler	*Limnothlypis swainsonii*
Ovenbird	*Seiurus aurocapillus*
Northern Waterthrush	*Seiurus noveboracensis*
Louisiana Waterthrush	*Seiurus motacilla*
Kentucky Warbler	*Oporornis formosus*
Connecticut Warbler	*Oporornis agilis*
Mourning Warbler	*Oporornis philadelphia*
Common Yellowthroat	*Geothlypis trichas*
Gray-crowned Yellowthroat	*Geothlypis poliocephala*
Hooded Warbler	*Wilsonia citrina*
Wilson's Warbler	*Wilsonia pusilla*
Canada Warbler	*Wilsonia canadensis*
Golden-crowned Warbler	*Basileuterus culicivorus*
Rufous-capped Warbler	*Basileuterus rufifrons*
Golden-browed Warbler	*Basileuterus belli*
Yellow-breasted Chat	*Icteria virens*
Gray-throated Chat	*Granatellus sallaei*

Genera *incertae sedis*

Bananaquit	*Coereba flaveola*

Tanagers—*Thraupidae*

Common Bush-Tanager	*Chlorospingus opthalmicus*
Gray-headed Tanager	*Eucometis penicillata*
Black-throated Shrike-Tanager	*Lanio aurantius*
Red-crowned Ant-Tanager	*Habia rubica*
Red-throated Ant-Tanager	*Habia fuscicauda*
Rose-throated Tanager	*Piranga roseogularis*
Hepatic Tanager	*Piranga flava*
Summer Tanager	*Piranga rubra*
Scarlet Tanager	*Piranga olivacea*
Western Tanager	*Piranga ludoviciana*
Flame-colored Tanager	*Piranga bidentata*
White-winged Tanager	*Piranga leucoptera*
Crimson-collared Tanager	*Ramphocelus sanguinolentus*
Passerini's Tanager	*Ramphocelus passerinii*
Blue-gray Tanager	*Thraupis episcopus*
Yellow-winged Tanager	*Thraupis abbas*
Golden-hooded Tanager	*Tangara larvata*
Rufous-winged Tanager	*Tangara lavinia*
Green Honeycreeper	*Chlorophanes spiza*
Shining Honeycreeper	*Cyanerpes lucidus*
Red-legged Honeycreeper	*Cyanerpes cyaneus*

Seedeaters and Sparrows—*Emberizidae*

Blue-black Grassquit	*Volatinia jacarina*
Slate-colored Seedeater	*Sporophila schistacea*
Variable Seedeater	*Sporophila americana*
White-collared Seedeater	*Sporophila torqueola*
Thick-billed Seed-Finch	*Oryzoborus funereus*
Blue Seedeater	*Amaurospiza concolor*
Yellow-faced Grassquit	*Tiaris olivacea*
Grassland Yellow-Finch	*Sicalis luteola*
Orange-billed Sparrow	*Arremon aurantiirostris*
Olive Sparrow	*Arremonops rufivirgatus*
Green-backed Sparrow	*Arremonops chloronotus*
Botteri's Sparrow	*Aimophila botterii*
Rusty Sparrow	*Aimophila rufescens*
Chipping Sparrow	*Spizella passerina*
Clay-colored Sparrow	*Spizella allida*

141

Vesper Sparrow	*Pooecetes gramineus*
Lark Sparrow	*Chondestes grammacus*
Savannah Sparrow	*Passerculus sandwichensis*
Grasshopper Sparrow	*Ammodramus savannarum*
Lincoln's Sparrow	*Melospiza lincolnii*
White-throated Sparrow	*Zonotrichia albicollis*
White-crowned Sparrow	*Zonotrichia leucophrys*

Saltators, Grosbeaks and Buntings—Cardinalidae

Grayish Saltator	*Saltator coerulescens*
Buff-throated Saltator	*Saltator maximus*
Black-headed Saltator	*Saltator atriceps*
Black-faced Grosbeak	*Caryothraustes poliogaster*
Northern Cardinal	*Cardinalis cardinalis*
Rose-breasted Grosbeak	*Pheucticus ludovicianus*
Blue-black Grosbeak	*Cyanocompsa cyanoides*
Blue Bunting	*Cyanocompsa parellina*
Blue Grosbeak	*Guiraca caerulea*
Lazuli Bunting	*Passerina amoena*
Indigo Bunting	*Passerina cyanea*
Painted Bunting	*Passerina ciris*
Dickcissel	*Spiza americana*

Blackbirds—*Icteridae*

Bobolink	*Dolichonyx oryzivorus*
Red-winged Blackbird	*Agelaius phoeniceus*
Eastern Meadowlark	*Sturnella magna*
Yellow-headed Blackbird	*Xanthocephalus xanthocephalus*
Melodious Blackbird	*Dives dives*
Great-tailed Grackle	*Quiscalus mexicanus*
Bronzed Cowbirdth	*Molothrus aeneus*
Brown-headed Cowbird	*Molothrus ater*
Giant Cowbird	*Molothrus oryzivorus*
Black-cowled Oriole	*Icterus prosthemelas*
Orchard Oriole	*Icterus spurius*
Hooded Oriole	*Icterus cucullatus*
Yellow-backed Oriole	*Icterus chrysater*
Yellow-tailed Oriole	*Icterus mesomelas*
Orange Oriole	*Icterus auratus*
Altamira Oriole	*Icterus gularis*
Audubon's Oriole	*Icterus graduacauda*

Baltimore Oriole	*Icterus galbula*
Yellow-billed Cacique	*Amblycercus holosericeus*
Chestnut-headed Oropendola	*Psarocolius wagleri*
Montezuma Oropendola	*Psarocolius montezuma*

Finches, Crossbills and Allies—*Fringillidae*

Scrub Euphonia	*Euphonia affinis*
Yellow-throated Euphonia	*Euphonia hirundinacea*
Elegant Euphonia	*Euphonia elegantissima*
Olive-backed Euphonia	*Euphonia gouldi*
White-vented Euphonia	*Euphonia minuta*
Red-Crossbill	*Loxia curvirostra*
Black-headed Siskin	*Carduelis notata*
Lesser Goldfinch	*Carduelis psaltria*

Old World Sparrows—*Passeridae*

House Sparrow	*Passer domesticus*

143

Index

144

147

149

Message from Belize Audubon Society

It is another milestone for us at the Belize Audubon Society (BAS) to be joining forces with Carolyn Miller, National Audubon Society, Alejandro Grajal, Fernando Zavala, Philip Balderamos, and Judy Lumb to produce another wonderful publication that highlights 101 "princesses of biodiversity", as birds have been referred to. In our 2009-2013 Strategic Plan, BAS has established a new programme that aims at focusing on biodiversity conservation, particularly avian conservation. This programme is a reflection of the Society's historical dedication to the conservation of birds. When the organization began 40 years ago in 1969, indeed bird-watching was one of the primary activities that influenced our growth and development. Our logo was developed depicting the relationship between the frigate bird and the booby bird, a common sighting at Half Moon Caye Natural Monument, home to a rookery of red-footed booby birds and a key protected area managed by the Society

Today, we continue to champion conservation of birds and identification of Important Bird Areas in Belize. These areas will further enhance the protected areas system as they serve to link people and birds. As one of the leaders in protected areas management, the BAS manages nine protected areas in Belize, including management of one of Belize's two Ramsar Sites and an Important Bird Area, the Crooked Tree Wildlife Sanctuary, home to many bird species recorded in Belize. Protected areas management has extended the organization's mandate to broader sustainable natural resources management, in addition to strengthening the organization's role of promoting the conservation of biodiversity especially birds and their habitats

The Belize Audubon Society, as the BirdLife Partner in Belize, looks forward to working with both its international and national partners in the continued conservation of birds and their habitats and also link people with conservation. It is our hope that *101 Birds of Belize* will further build awareness of birds of Belize and promote a greater appreciation of the role that birds play in our daily lives, whether as an icon figure on our dollar bills, as a major attraction to tourists, or simply another creature with a right

to existence. We hope that this book will strengthen bird conservation efforts in Belize and we are extremely grateful to all who contributed to making this book a reality.

Anna D. Hoare
BAS Executive Director

151